T0219841

CLOUD COMPUTING BASICS

A NON-TECHNICAL INTRODUCTION

Anders Lisdorf

Apress®

Cloud Computing Basics: A Non-Technical Introduction

Anders Lisdorf
Copenhagen, Denmark

ISBN-13 (pbk): 978-1-4842-6920-6   ISBN-13 (electronic): 978-1-4842-6921-3
https://doi.org/10.1007/978-1-4842-6921-3

Managing Director, Apress Media LLC: Welmoed Spahr
Acquisitions Editor: Susan McDermott
Development Editor: Laura Berendson
Coordinating Editor: Rita Fernando

Cover designed by eStudioCalamar

Distributed to the book trade worldwide by Springer Science+Business Media New York, 1 New York Plaza, New York, NY 100043. Phone 1-800-SPRINGER, fax (201) 348-4505, e-mail orders-ny@springer-sbm.com, or visit www.springeronline.com. Apress Media, LLC is a California LLC and the sole member (owner) is Springer Science + Business Media Finance Inc (SSBM Finance Inc). SSBM Finance Inc is a **Delaware** corporation.

For information on translations, please e-mail booktranslations@springernature.com; for reprint, paperback, or audio rights, please e-mail bookpermissions@springernature.com.

Apress titles may be purchased in bulk for academic, corporate, or promotional use. eBook versions and licenses are also available for most titles. For more information, reference our Print and eBook Bulk Sales web page at http://www.apress.com/bulk-sales.

Any source code or other supplementary material referenced by the author in this book is available to readers on GitHub via the book's product page, located at www.apress.com/9781484269206. For more detailed information, please visit http://www.apress.com/source-code.

Printed on acid-free paper

This book is dedicated to the memory of my father, Bent Lisdorf, who passed away while I was writing this book. He and his dedication to freedom, solidarity, and humanitarian action will be missed by anyone who knew him.

Contents

About the Author

Anders Lisdorf has worked with bridging on-premise and cloud technologies for more than a decade in many different types of companies and industries. The last few years he has been working as a consultant helping a variety of customers transition to the cloud. He is also an experienced entrepreneur, building cloud native Software as a Service products.

About the Technical Reviewers

Lars Rosenberg Nielsen is an expert in cloud computing, often working in consulting roles as a cloud solution architect, a DevOps engineer, an enterprise architect, and a trusted technical advisor for executives. Lars has extensive hands-on experience from technical engagements in customer-facing roles in areas of cloud native architecture, cloud strategy, migration and platforms, architectural design, engineering, digital transformation, DevOps, and information technology. Lars holds several advanced-level cloud, Kubernetes, and architecture certifications.

Stanislav Novoseletskiy is a regional director of data and AI at Microsoft. He is a strong believer in positive change and transformation. His career began in 1997 as a helpdesk engineer, then he was promoted to an application developer, then to database developer, and eventually became a SQL DBA. He joined Microsoft in 2006 and has held various technical and sales roles aligned with helping businesses and governments transform and evolve with the use of data and insights.

Acknowledgments

A book, at least a quality book, is never the work of a single person. Neither is this one. I have been fortunate to receive help and guidance from incredibly qualified and dedicated people. First, I want to thank the Apress team for guidance and input. Susan McDermott for making me think hard about the structure and direction of the book and Rita Fernando for the incredibly sharp observations keeping me honest and to the point as well as more than a few suggestions that have significantly improved the book. Reviewers Stanislav Novoseletskiy and Lars Rosenberg Nielsen have similarly challenged me and made good suggestions for improving the content and making it clearer. I also want to thank Ole Kjeldsen for sharing his deep knowledge and experience with the cloud in general and Microsoft in particular. Mogens Nørgaard provided me with many hours of stimulating discussions about the cloud, data, and security. Through his intimate knowledge of the history and technology of Oracle, he provided me with a deeper understanding that would have been hard won from published resources.

In the course of the last decade, I have also learned a lot from colleagues and other acquaintances, both practical and theoretical. They are unfortunately too many to mention here but be sure that I am grateful for all our discussions.

Above all, I want to thank my father, during whose prolonged illness and eventual death this book was written. He was always there for me. Without his love and guidance, I would never have been able to write this book.

It should be noted that even if I have been blessed with quality help and suggestions from all these people, everything in this book is my responsibility and they cannot be blamed in any way for any shortcomings of this manuscript.

Introduction

Ever since my childhood I had a fascination with clouds. Real clouds up in the sky, white and fluffy or gray and gloomy, afforded an ever-present drama unfolding above for the curious spectator looking toward the heavens, as inquisitive children are wont to do. Maybe it was because of ample exposure to the perennial cloudiness of my native West Denmark with its rich variety and texture across seasons, but I always found clouds to be mysterious and captivating.

Today my interest is intact, although the clouds I study are no longer up in the sky but somewhere in cyberspace, even if following them doesn't afford the same ever-present drama. This book is about understanding the language and logic of cloud computing, what technologies are available and the nature of the vendors who supply them, and how the economy and security of the cloud and working with it impacts an organization. It is an attempt to explain and describe the basics for interested readers with little or no technical background to get an overview of what the cloud is and be able to participate in intelligent discussions about how to use it.

My own way into cloud computing has followed an uneven path. By the mid to end 2000s, the cloud was emerging as an interesting new technology. I was working as an enterprise architect and started to look into what this new thing had to offer. The cloud caught on as the go-to marketing buzzword and quickly it assumed a meaning equivalent to fairy dust, which when sprinkled on any technological solution, would magically transform it and make it better in all discernible ways.

A few years later I founded my own startup, which delivered a Software as a Service (SaaS) product built entirely on cloud infrastructure, which demonstrated to me the power of the cloud. No need to buy servers and rent rooms to set them up and run them. This was the first proof for me that although the cloud was not quite fairy dust, it was definitely the future. Even if it wasn't decidedly easy, it was not as hard as just a few years earlier to build a company from scratch entirely in the cloud.

Fast forward about a decade, and I found myself in the United States serving the city of New York by helping them deliver on an ambitious new cloud-first strategy, again as an enterprise architect. For all new development it should first be considered if it could be built in the cloud. This was a fascinating transition to the cloud that many modern companies of any scale are finding themselves in. These experiences alerted me to many of the themes and practical insights that have informed this book.

Over the course of more than a decade, I have had the privilege of working with all five big cloud vendors to some extent and a few of the smaller ones. It is interesting to see the emerging patterns and how they all have something valuable to offer.

As a side note, I have chosen to focus on what I call the big five cloud vendors: AWS, Google Cloud Platform, IBM cloud, Microsoft Azure, and Oracle. There are other vendors out there, and I encourage you to explore them on your own.

The trajectory of the cloud since the end of the 2000s until now follows the consultancy Gartner's so called "hype cycle." It started at the peak of inflated expectations and went down through the trough of disillusionment and is now on its way up toward the plateau of productivity. Getting caught up in the hype is easy, but to really understand and appreciate the transformative power of the cloud in starting a new business or running an established business of any size, let us consider a thought experiment where we are starting the same business in 2005 and in 2020.

Imagine you are starting an online store. First you need a website in order to start selling. If you want to start small, you can go down to your local electronics store and buy a few PCs. If you want to start bigger, you order a rack and computers from a wholesale supplier. Next you have to find out where to put these computers. If you don't already have a spare room, you have to rent that spare room somewhere. In the beginning you might get away with just that but quickly you would need to buy additional machines and rent a similar room somewhere else in order to have a backup site in case the first one fails. If you don't have a backup and there is a fire or flood, your entire business would be gone with the computers. Speaking of fire, don't forget to install a fire suppression system for your server rooms. But these are not the typical sprinkler systems, since water would damage your machines just the same as fire. These are highly specialized systems based on a mixture of gases and chemicals. On top of this you have to carry out fire drills. Of course you could say that this is excessive and not necessary, but try to explain to the venture capital fund you are pitching a $5 million investment to that if there were a fire, their entire investment would be gone.

I think at this point you can see that even before you can start building your shop and website, you have to invest a lot of time and money to just get started. When you are ready, you need to buy licenses for software for the web shop and other supporting business functions like accounting, salary, warehouse management, HR, and marketing.

When all that is paid, you have to hire and maintain a team of operations specialists to maintain, upgrade, and patch all the software that you just bought.

Not only do you have high upfront costs to purchase hardware and software, but you also have monthly costs for data center rental and operational staff even before you start selling anything.

Now, contrast this with starting the same company in 2020. The first thing to decide now is not where and what equipment to purchase, but how much of the technology stack you want to be responsible for yourself. You could just go to a site like Shopify and configure it there. The ERP system and other software to support salary, a call center, and customer support are all similarly available instantly and configurable. All of this will typically run for a fixed monthly fee.

If you want more control or have more specific requirements that are not served by these standard systems, you could still procure the servers you need, but now that can be done instantly from cloud providers. You can often even choose them preinstalled with the business software you want. You don't have to rent rooms in multiple locations and install fire suppression systems; you just configure your servers to be in different data centers of the cloud provider. Even in this scenario there is no upfront cost and everything can be run for a monthly fee.

Whichever route you take in the cloud today, you can start your company over your morning coffee at Starbucks and have it up and running in the afternoon over mojitos at California Pizza Kitchen while waiting for your chicken tequila fettuccine.

This applies not only to online shops but to virtually any type of company or organization at any scale. The specifics of the benefits will differ and depend, but the potential is there for anyone. However, to benefit and harness this potential, it is necessary to understand the cloud and how it works. This is what we will do in this book.

- **Chapter 1, Cloud Foundations,** lays the foundation for understanding what the cloud is. We look at the history of the concept to understand where it comes from. But understanding the term is not the same as understanding the concept, which is why we investigate how best to conceptualize it.

- **Chapter 2, Why Cloud?,** provides an overview of the future of cloud computing and an account of the major drivers for organizations to move to the cloud. Economy is a common one, but security, agility, scalability, and sustainability are other drivers. These drivers are not equally relevant to all organizations, but there is something for everyone.

- **Chapter 3, The Genealogy of Cloud Computing,** is a history of different technical developments that led to the cloud in its present version. The traces go back deep in history and help explain certain features that may at first appear puzzling.

- **Chapters 4 to 8** introduce the major players in the cloud industry: IBM, Oracle, Microsoft, Amazon, and Google. The vast majority of customers will end up using cloud solutions from one of these five major cloud vendors. Understanding their history, target groups, strengths, and weaknesses makes it possible to select a better choice of fit between an organization and vendor.

- **Chapter 9, Cloud Vendor Profiles,** compares the big five cloud vendors on five key parameters—customer orientation, vision, product packaging, end user target, and cloud focus—in order to analyze the key differences between them.

  The cloud impacts many different areas, but four stand out: technology, security, economy, and work. The next four chapters dive into each of these to describe in more detail how the cloud impacts them.

- **Chapter 10, Cloud Technology,** presents an overview of SaaS, PaaS, and IaaS. The infrastructure services section dives into the first of the three major categories of cloud services. These are the ones close to a traditional data center and are particularly versatile. We see how the basic features of a network—compute and storage—are being packaged as services to be consumed. There is a high degree of uniformity across vendors in this category. Platform services present more integrated and focused functionality like databases and messaging solutions used by applications. These services abstract the basic infrastructure services and can be used without having to worry about most operational processes like upgrades and patching. Here, functionality starts to diverge a bit more. We focus on a few sub-categories. Software services talks about the category closest to the end users. We see examples of this and look into the major subcategories where SaaS is employed at scale. These differ most across vendors and allow for little individual tailoring.

- **Chapter 11, Securing the Cloud**, focuses on the main aspects of what it takes to secure the cloud. We look at it from a holistic risk-based angle and go through the different classes of services and features that cloud platforms usually offer to increase security in the cloud.

- **Chapter 12, Cloud Economy,** touches on how the economy of the cloud differs and how it needs to be approached. In this chapter we look at the possibilities that exist for managing and optimizing the economy in the cloud. There are different features that allow the organization to get insight into and control the economy of cloud deployments.

- **Chapter 13, Working with the Cloud**, looks into how the cloud impacts work in a traditional IT department. We describe how the cloud affects the job market. Because usage of the cloud is expanding rapidly, it is changing the skills needed in the contemporary job market. Cloud skills are already in short supply. A number of new roles appear, and old roles are being adapted to the cloud. Another thing to keep in mind is that traditional roles are being redefined, which necessitates retooling and an effort of employees to get out of their comfort zone.

The final chapter helps the reader put the book into an actionable perspective.

- **Chapter 14, Adopting the Cloud**, will provide a number of patterns of adoption at the organizational level. Not all organizations can spring forth as cloud-native like the hotshot startups that have captured the agenda of cloud computing so far. Many companies are much more selective and constrained in their adoption. This chapter describes how organizations can approach cloud adoption in a structured and proven way. The goal is to describe the most common ways organizations can approach cloud computing.

The book can be read in a sequence. Chapters 1-2 can be read as an introduction to the cloud for the non-technical reader seeking a primer. This will give you a basic understanding of the cloud as a computing phenomenon and the impact of the key aspects of economy, security, and work.

Chapters 3-10 provide an overview focused on the technical aspects of the cloud that allows readers with an interest in technical perspectives to orient themselves in the modern world of cloud computing. Chapters 11-14 can be read in isolation by managers at any level who are responsible for managing or adopting cloud technologies. Those chapters introduce the most important themes relevant to creating a strategy for cloud computing.

Cloud Foundations

In this chapter, we lay the foundation for understanding what the cloud actually is. We start by considering the history of the term. Then we look at how to define it in order to get a firmer handle on what we mean by cloud computing. We also investigate different ways to conceptualize the cloud. It has, for example, been suggested that the cloud is a utility or a service, which highlights certain important aspects of the cloud but also mischaracterizes it in other ways. The chapter seeks to establish an understanding of what it means when we talk about the *cloud*.

The History of the Term "Cloud"

Many ideas come together in the cloud. They can be traced from multiple sources, which we do in a later chapter, but the origin of the term "cloud" in itself is to many people a bit mysterious. Why would a cloud convey an idea about technology being accessed through a network? The idea of a communication network precedes the talk of the cloud. The first mention of the cloud was in the 90s, but before that it was already customary for engineers to use a cloud to denote a network.

© Anders Lisdorf 2021
A. Lisdorf, *Cloud Computing Basics*,
https://doi.org/10.1007/978-1-4842-6921-3_1

Why a Cloud?

To understand why the cloud metaphor came to denote the technological revolution we are now seeing, we have to look at what a network actually is from an engineering perspective. When you connect multiple computers in a network, this happens through multiple nodes. These are computers or other electronic devices that have the capability to connect to other devices or computers and route communication traffic between computers. Every node in the network does little more than receive data from one end point and route it to another. The familiar radio towers that we see if we look hard around us are all just such nodes that form a network that our cell phones can use to connect to other cell phones.

The identity and connections of these nodes, how they route traffic, is not important in order to understand the properties of the network. If you had to describe how one cell phone connects to another in a diagram, it would be inconvenient to document all the radio towers that form the network through which these phones communicate.

Rather than try to capture all these details and entities that constitute the network, a metaphor was needed to symbolize an amorphous collection of machines. What better symbol of something amorphous than a cloud? This was also relatively easy to sketch out by hand. Engineers often communicate ideas by drawing sketches on whiteboards or on paper. Drawing a cloud was a convenient and fast way to illustrate that something connected to a network to which other things were connected as well.

The Origin of the Term "Cloud"

The first public mention of the cloud was, as far as we can tell, in 1994 in a *Wired* article by author and journalist Steven Levy. The article was about a company called General Magic. The company was founded by the creators of the Macintosh computer, Bill Atkinson and Andy Herzfeld. By 1994, they had spent four years trying to create an ambitious new communications platform to change everyone's life. They imagined that "a lot of different areas are converging on an electronic box that's in your pocket, that's with you all the time, that supports you in some way." Obviously at that time no "electronic box" would be able to do much computing that would be very interesting, so that had to be done on a server to which the device connected through a network. The product General Magic envisioned was called Telescript and was the interface people would use to connect. It was a system to tie together all sorts of different networks into one standardized interface. They imagined that:

"Now, instead of just having a device to program, we now have the entire Cloud out there, where a single program can go and travel to many different sources of information and create sort of a virtual service".

—Bill and Andy's Excellent Adventure II, *Wired* 1994

It is interesting that in this quote we see not only the word "cloud" but also clearly the contours of the concept of the cloud: the ability to access information and functionality from any device at any location.

The particular technology offered by General Magic, however, did not catch on. Even though they were visionaries in the field, the company ceased operations and was liquidated at the start of the 2000s, before cloud computing really caught on. The word "cloud" was not adopted by the general public immediately.

It wasn't until 1996 that a major company took the concept and word to heart and built a strategy on it. At the time, the Internet and browsers like Netscape were catching on. Internet business was the hot thing. In an office park at the outskirts of Houston, Texas, a group of technology executives built a new strategy for their company based on exactly that assumption.

Marketing executive Steve Favoloro and technologist Sean O'Sullivan envisioned that business software and file storage would move to the Internet and they were scheming on how their company, Compaq, would benefit from this. This was the start of a multibillion-dollar business selling servers to Internet providers. It is uncertain exactly which of the two, Favoloro or O'Sullivan, came up with the term, but it is found in an internal document titled "Internet Solutions Division Strategy for Cloud Computing" from November 14, 1996. Although the term cloud was conceptualized as a marketing effort, Compaq eventually decided against using the term in part due to concerns from the PR department.

Sean O'Sullivan went on to build an online educational services company, NetCentric, in 1997. He even filed a trademark application for the term "cloud computing," which would have been convenient for him today, had it gone through. But it did not.

Compaq profited greatly from the strategy by selling hardware to support this new cloud thing and the Internet as well as "proto cloud" services like web-based email. In addition, the cloud computing juggernaut, Salesforce, was founded in 1999. Even so, the cloud didn't really catch on as a term.

It wasn't until 10 years later, in 2006, that the term reached prime time. Eric Schmidt introduced the term at the Search Engine Strategies Conference:

> *"What's interesting [now] is that there is an emergent new model, and you all are here because you are part of that new model. I don't think people have really understood how big this opportunity really is. It starts with the premise that the data services and architecture should be on servers. We call it cloud computing – they should be in a 'cloud' somewhere".*

—Conversation with Eric Schmidt hosted by Danny Sullivan

Here for the first time the full scope of the term was introduced. Major technology companies that would later develop into key cloud vendors, such as Amazon, Microsoft, and IBM, started using the term as well. The following year an article in *The New York Times* cemented the term in the public eye, with the headline: "IBM to Push 'Cloud Computing,' Using Data from Afar" in the November 15, 2007 issue. From that time, the use of the term, as well as the industry itself, has gone just one way: up.

The Birth of the Cloud Computing Concept

The use of the term "cloud" started as a convenient way to refer to an abstracted network used by engineers. Once people realized that computing and data storage would move the individual devices onto centralized servers, the abstraction of the network access from those individual servers came to conveniently denote the whole concept of the cloud. Another important aspect is that the term was conceived from a marketing perspective and used as a general term to describe very different solutions that all had one thing in common: the use of the Internet. Today it is such a common term that we talk about cloud stocks, see it referred to casually in movies and frequently in headlines in the general stream of news media. It has become a mainstream term that most people have some vague understanding of, but in order to get a firmer grip of the concept and technologies that power this term, we need to narrow it down and consider it with some more precision.

Definitions of Cloud Computing

While definitions are not truths about the world, they are important sources for understanding how certain aspects of the world are conceptualized.

The IT consultancy Gartner was one of the first to define cloud computing in 2008. It has subsequently been slightly updated:

"Cloud computing is a style of computing in which scalable and elastic IT-enabled capabilities are delivered as a service using Internet technologies."

—Gartner Glossary

This definition points to some of the key aspects of cloud computing: scalability, elasticity, and delivered as a service over the Internet. Scalability aims at the property of the cloud in contrast to on-premise computing that ramping up computing and storage is very easy. You don't have to order machines, unwrap them, and connect them to your data center. Anything is easily scaled up. Elasticity, on the other hand, aims at the fact that this scalability goes both ways: it will also scale down when capacity is no longer needed.

Later we go deeper into the importance of the service concept in cloud computing. This definition is quite open and draws the contours of the cloud, but it does not tell us a lot of specifics.

A more precise and comprehensive definition is the one by The National Institute of Standards in Technology (NIST). Virtually every exposition of cloud refers to this definition and it has become the de facto standard definition of what is and what is not cloud. Therefore, it may be a good idea to look into its background.

One of the key focus areas of NIST is to make standards to further innovation, especially for government agencies. Under the Obama administration there was a push for transitioning from the costly hosting and licensing models of the prevailing on-premise computing to the promise of the cheaper and more flexible cloud. However, that did not come by itself. It was difficult for agencies as well as private companies at the time to distinguish old fashioned hosting from cloud computing. At the time the definition was finished, the purpose was clearly stated by NIST computer scientist Peter Mell:

"When agencies or companies use this definition (..) they have a tool to determine the extent to which the information technology implementations they are considering meet the cloud characteristics and models. This is important because by adopting an authentic cloud, they are more likely to reap the promised benefits of cloud—cost savings, energy savings, rapid deployment, and customer empowerment"

—NIST press release, October 2011

The work had been going on for more than three years through 15 drafts. The structure of the definition is around three sections:

- *Essential characteristics*—Described five key characteristics that defined cloud computing: On-demand self-service, broad network access, resource pooling, rapid elasticity, and measured service.

- *Service models*—Concerned with the different ways cloud resources could be consumed: Software as a Service (SaaS), Platform as a Service (PaaS), and Infrastructure as a Service (IaaS).

- *Deployment models*—About how cloud infrastructure could be provisioned.

Although this formed the basic vocabulary of the cloud and is still used as the definition of cloud, there are certain aspects that bear witness to the specific time and context and may no longer be as useful. Let's look at the three sections to understand what was meant by them and how relevant they are today.

Essential Characteristics

The essential characteristics were meant as the properties a cloud solution should have. If it did not have the following five characteristics, it was not considered a cloud solution.

On-demand self-service highlights the need for the end user to be able to provision computing resources by themselves. This was in contrast to the typical model at the time of hosting by one of the large hosting providers or on-premise. To provision computing infrastructure at the time, it was necessary to order servers and software from vendors or hosting companies. This was a slow process that did not align with the wish for agility and flexibility. It should not be necessary to involve anybody else as you would do when submitting a purchase order and waiting for someone to execute it. It should happen automatically. Today some of the biggest cloud vendors have services that need to be activated on request, which can take a while.

Broad network access in practice refers basically to services being available through the Internet since most cloud computing is public cloud. Basically, anyone with a laptop, table, or cell phone should be able to access the computing resources. This characteristic rules out an on-premise data center behind a company firewall. The network access needs not be Internet. There could be other types of ways to connect to the cloud, which we are beginning see in the area of IoT (Internet of Things). It has also become common for cloud providers to provide a dedicated fiber connection between the customer and provider data center. Some vendors also offer their cloud services in "boxes" that are completely cut off from any network.

Resource pooling has more to do with how you achieve the effect. The intent here is to say that in cloud computing, several users use the same pool of computing infrastructure. They don't get one computer each. Without this the goal of energy savings would not be realized. This is still important, but in practice it is possible through cloud providers to gain access to single dedicated machines, sometimes called bare metal or dedicated instance. Consequently, this is not in practice an essential characteristic.

Rapid elasticity may at first seem a bit odd, because how do elasticity and silicon computers fit together? Obviously, the point is not that the computers should bend around corners. The meaning is metaphorical. If a service like a website suddenly has a lot more users because of a flash sale, for example, it needs to be able to scale up the computing power to handle this quickly. Then, when the sale is over, it should scale back down like an elastic band that stretches and retracts when force is no longer applied. Here it is important to be aware that not all cloud services come with this automatically. Rather it often needs to be built by the customer.

Measured service basically means that the customer should only pay for what they use to avoid paying for a machine standing idle in a data center. This should be transparent to the customer. In practice the unit used to measure can differ greatly. It could be time, storage, processing capacity, number of users, number of instructions, or any other measurable property of relevance to the service. The most common are time and number of users. In practice vendors are not always making it as transparent, as NIST would have wanted them to. It can be very difficult or impossible for a customer to validate the correctness of the metering.

Although these characteristics were helpful a decade ago for distinguishing between old-fashioned hosting and this new cloud thing, the lines are more blurred today. In practice, these characteristics are good guidelines of what you can expect from most cloud solutions today, but they are not an accurate reflection of all cloud computing. It is perhaps better to think of these characteristics as common characteristics that we would expect to find most often. If, say, only two apply we would be hard pressed to call the service a cloud service, but if three or four applies it is clearer. It is important also to understand that it does not necessarily detract from the solution when it does not fulfill all criteria. For example, having a dedicated instance reserved for a year or two is much cheaper. Also, connecting through a direct connection to the cloud vendor's data center rather than through the Internet is a crucial piece of infrastructure that drives adoption of cloud computing. These solutions do not fit all the essential characteristics.

Service Models

The three service models have become standard parlance in modern cloud computing, even if the boundaries between them are breaking down. They all rely on the service concept, which we look into in more detail at a later point.

- **Software as a Service (SaaS)** is a model where everything is managed by the vendor. You cannot program anything yourself, you only configure and use it through a web browser. Common examples are Google's services like Docs, Calendar, and Sheets or Microsoft's Office 365. These provide the user with only limited options to configure the software. Many enterprise applications fall into this category, like SAP's SuccessFactors, Oracle HCM, ServiceNow, Zendesk, and more.

- **Platform as a Service (PaaS)** is a bit less straightforward and the examples are more heterogeneous. This service model refers to platforms that can be used to program applications by the consumer. It is possible to write code and configure the service, but the vendor manages the underlying infrastructure.

- **Infrastructure as a Service (IaaS)** is the most basic form where basic computing resources are provided and the consumer installs and manages the needed software. This model gives the most control but also requires the most work.

Although these are good ideal types, there are new models that fall somewhere in between. For example, so called serverless computing or Function as a Service (FaaS), which is the capability of being able to write a piece of code that executes based on triggers, like a web service call. This is somewhere between PaaS and SaaS. Another example is containers, which are a level above the operating system and somewhere between IaaS and PaaS. Some types of software come in all variants, like databases. You can install a database on an IaaS machine, use the same database as a PaaS offering and, in some cases, even as a SaaS product. It is sometimes contested whether it is one or the other. Consequently, it is important to look at the service in question and evaluate whether it fits the needs more than whether it fits the label.

Deployment Models

There are different ways to deploy cloud infrastructures or more accurately, different ways to allow access to them. The deployment models specify different types of clouds.

- **Private cloud** is when the cloud services are offered on a private infrastructure. Although this is certainly a theoretical option and some organizations have made headway into offering a limited array of cloud services as a private cloud to internal developers, this is not a widespread model and misses most if not all of the benefits of the cloud. It is essentially just another way of running an on-premise data center.

- **Community cloud** is when a specific community of consumers band together to build a cloud that they can use similar, to a private club cloud. This is also a theoretical possibility. It was much more commonly talked about a decade ago, but today little cloud computing is deployed in this way. I have not been able to verify any existing large-scale deployments of this type. If you stretch the definition, it could be argued that the large cloud vendors' so-called GovClouds act as community clouds. Subsets of their cloud offerings are tailor made to government customers, so they might fit this description. However, they also fit the description of a specific variant of a public cloud.

- **Public cloud** is the common model that we all know. Virtually all cloud computing today is deployed according to this model. A user can access and use this through the public Internet. The difference between now and when the definition was made is perhaps increased capabilities for keeping the public cloud private with the aid of data encryption in transit and at rest.

- **Hybrid cloud** is a combination of two or more of these models. Because the first two are mostly theoretical constructs, this one is also irrelevant at least in its NIST formulation. The idea of a hybrid cloud in a different sense however is much more common, since most organizations run hybrid infrastructures with multiple cloud providers and their own (non-cloud) data centers. In a sense, the hybrid cloud is very widespread. Just not in the original definition offered by NIST.

Toward a Concept of the Cloud

As you can see from the previous sections, the definition of the cloud is not as clear-cut as that of say a carbon atom. There are a number of aspects that are commonly associated with cloud products but in specific cases some of them can be lacking and still "count" as cloud-based. We saw that the characteristics were more common than essential and that it is a fluctuating landscape. Rather than come up with a clear-cut definition that will never receive agreement, we are better served to try to understand the cloud phenomenon and the market that drives its development, which is the subject of the next chapter. In the remainder of this chapter, we focus on a few concepts that are key to understanding what is special about the cloud and how it is conceptualized. These concepts are utility, service, and layers.

The Cloud as a Utility

Along with the taming of electricity came the modern concept of a utility as a way to deliver a service to the public. It is important to notice that we are not talking about the economic concept of utility as a measure of worth. We are talking about a public utility—like gas, electricity, and water—that is offered to consumers in a standardized way. A public utility is not necessarily a governmental institution. It can be, and often is, privately owned. It maintains an infrastructure that offers a public service its consumers.

The idea that computing could be a utility arose, as so many other key ideas, in the 60s. John McCarthy, speaking at the MIT Centennial in 1961, said:

> *"(..) computing may some day be organized as a public utility just as the telephone system is a public utility... The computer utility could become the basis of a new and important industry."*

> —Architects of the Information Society

This can be seen as a rallying cry for what we today call cloud computing. In many ways this vision of computing as a utility has come true, but in other ways it is also a misleading metaphor for what cloud computing is and how it works.

There is no clear definition of what a public utility is. However, most definitions just assert that it is an organization that provides a basic service to the public and ends up listing the typical cases like water, gas, electricity, and transportation. Let's therefore try to compare a few aspects of traditional utilities and cloud computing.

Product

If a utility offers gas, that is what you get. No more, no less. Similar for water, you get just water. The product being offered is undifferentiated and the consumer has no options to choose from. It could be said that for telephony, it differs somewhat. Still, when you buy a cell phone connection, even though you can get different plans, you just get an undifferentiated connection. The difference in plans is more related to consumption patterns than the nature of the service, which remains a plain wireless connection. The method of consumption is similarly simple. For a typical utility, you just have to connect to the infrastructure and the product starts flowing. It will not stop until you discontinue the service or forget to pay the bills.

In the cloud, some individual services may offer a similar undifferentiated product such as storage, but the vast majority of services are not undifferentiated. Very little just starts flowing from the taps when you connect to the cloud. Even with a basic infrastructure service like computing, you have to decide on the type of CPU, memory, and operating system, and you often have to be ready to upgrade to secure service continuity. When it comes to Platform as a Service, there is even bigger differentiation: an MS SQL database is not the same as an Oracle database or a PostgreSQL database and these are even comparable relational databases that differ even more from other databases like graph databases.

For Software as a Service, there are very few if any similarities between the vendors. SAP HR, which is an HR system, differs significantly from Oracle HCM, which is also an HR system. Furthermore, anyone who has tried to implement an HR system can testify to the fact that the service doesn't just start flowing from the tap when you connect to it. It will often take months or even years before you can start using it, because it needs configuration and migration of data.

Path Dependency

In physics and mathematics, the concept of path dependency refers to a system whose state depends on the history of that system. If you heat a bowl of water, it will eventually boil regardless of how you heated it. This is not path-dependent. The same goes for other utilities: gas will come into your house given the right pressure regardless of where it came from or how it was treated. Utilities in general show no path dependency since the state of the system does not have to take into account any particular historical factors.

This is very rarely the case for cloud computing. It could be the case when you are starting something completely new. For example, when you build a new application. If you are transferring your HR system from one provider to another, there is path dependency in the configuration of the service. The state of the system reflects all the different HR events that have taken place in the system and is therefore path dependent. Almost all systems containing data in the cloud are consequently path dependent. Purely functional systems, like containers or some virtual machines, however, do not need to be path dependent if data is stored outside in a database for example and may be transferred easily to another provider. This is a key aspect that shows the limitations of the cloud as a utility. Data makes the cloud path dependent.

Transferability

The fact that utilities have no path dependency positively affects the transferability of a service. This allows the consumer to transfer to any provider without additional work. In the case of electricity or cell phone coverage, the consumer typically just has to sign the contract and will never know exactly when he or she transferred to the new provider.

The cloud, on the other hand, has path dependency for all data carrying applications. It is necessary to migrate the data to the new service because of this path dependency. This is actually a key parameter built into many vendors' business models that consumers are often wary of, namely vendor lock-in. The greater the vendor lockin, the less transferable the service. This is perhaps one of the biggest contrasts to the thinking of traditional utilities and their history of being regulated state monopolies. They had to be easily transferable in order to maintain competition. There is, however, a slow convergence toward higher transferability of certain types of services, especially from on-premise to the cloud but also between clouds. This only works when there is standardization and no path dependency.

Configuration

A utility like gas, water, and electricity needs no configuration. It is offered according to the specifications that are common in the service area. Water and gas will have a specific pressure and electricity a specific voltage and the consumer just needs to buy products that fit these specifications.

Again, this is very rarely the case in the cloud. Most services need to be configured in one way or another. Even with the simplest like storage, you have to decide what kind of storage you need. For higher-level SaaS products, the configuration takes on the scale of development of a new system, because there are so many parameters that need to be set before the service is operational. A customer typically has to hire a systems integrator for months to configure the service for use.

Service Continuity

For utilities, the service will never change. The electricity will remain the at same voltage. The water will remain water and will not become pink lemonade or Aperol spritz. The consumer will never have to do anything to adapt or to ensure service continuity. The utility will keep flowing without variance.

This is not the case in the cloud. Because it is software, it will in some cases need to be upgraded, which to varying degrees is up to the consumer. On this point, Software as a Service is better but new features will continually be made available, or the design will change, which will require the consumer to adapt. For other types of services, they will often become technically obsolete and be discontinued from the provider, which again requires the consumer to react in order to retain service continuity. This actually happens a lot faster than most organizations are used to running an on-premise data center. A database or machine will after all usually run until you turn it off, even if support has stopped for the product. This is not necessarily the case in the cloud.

Regulation

Utilities are often heavily regulated in terms of specifications for the service provided, such as water quality, and in terms of price or rules for transferability, in the case of cell phones. The reason for this is that often they have tended toward natural monopolies that need to be managed in order to maintain a competitive market. In the case of electricity, it is not feasible that a new market entrant can start building its own network, and the same is true for water and gas. If it belongs to a single corporation, they could take advantage of this monopoly to increase prices, which would harm the consumer.

Although the cloud is not a natural monopoly in the same way, it is close to it. It is not feasible for a new market entrant to start offering the same services as say AWS, and building the same infrastructure necessary to compete on that market. There is, however, competition from incumbents that we will look at later, but nothing restricts this handful of companies from agreeing tacitly or explicitly to a certain price because they together control a monopoly. Another complication compared to utilities and regulation is that cloud computing by its very nature is a global phenomenon and utilities have always been regulated at the national or state level. The same goes for quality of service. The consumer has very little power to complain since cloud offerings are often offered on a best effort basis. Consequently, the lack of regulation that traditional utilities have leaves the cloud consumer vulnerable.

Is the Cloud a Utility? Or More Like a Supermarket?

As can be seen in Table 1-1, many of the aspects we typically associate with a utility and perhaps what John McCarthy had in mind in the beginning of the 1960s are not comparable. The cloud may, in a select few cases, come close to properties that are typical of utilities, but in the big picture it would be wrong and misleading to think of the cloud as a utility.

Table 1-1. Comparison of Public Utilities and the Cloud

Aspect	Public Utility	Cloud
Product	Undifferentiated	Mostly differentiated but some undifferentiated products exist
Path dependency	No path dependency	All data carrying applications are path dependent, some functional ones are not
Transferability	Easily transferable	Mostly not easily transferable
Configuration	No configuration needed	Configuration needed before a service will be available
Service continuity	Consumer does not need to actively manage the service to retain service continuity	Customer needs to actively manage the service to retain service continuity
Regulation	Heavily regulated	Unregulated

That does not mean that the cloud is not valuable or cannot move more toward being a utility. It just means that if someone advertises the cloud as a utility, it makes sense to be critical and ask in what sense that is meant. Because by and large the cloud is not a utility.

A better way of thinking about the cloud is as a form of retail. In the retail industry, we have a handful of very large general-purpose retailers and many smaller specialized ones. If we think about fast-moving consumer goods, another pattern is important to be aware of. When we shop for groceries there is a range of products that are identical across the different supermarkets: milk, eggs, bacon, orange juice, beans, canned tomatoes, etc. The precise range is different from country to country. Not only are the products virtually identical with only the brand name differing, the price is too. These are the staples that draw customers into the store.

Retailers do not typically earn a lot if anything from these items, rather they earn their money on the other products that the customer grabs on the way to the register. These are more particular like vegan paleo granola or bacon ice cream. These products are difficult to compare and therefore more difficult for the consumer to evaluate in terms of price. Consequently, this is where the store makes the bulk of its profit.

Similarly, in the cloud there are consumer staples particularly in the Infrastructure as a Service world: virtual machines, blob storage, and block storage. These are offered with very little if any variation across the different cloud providers, and at a similar price. Then there are the more specialized offerings like the databases, security, and integration solutions. Because they differ more, it is difficult to compare the price and a higher mark-up can be made. Incidentally, the modern cloud market was created by a retailer, that is, Amazon with its Amazon Web Services. Subsequent entrants in this market have followed the same model.

When you think about it, this is also a better description of what cloud providers do. Retail is originally from the Old French word *tailler*, meaning "a piece cut off." Its modern meaning is "selling in smaller quantities." This precisely describes what cloud providers do. They buy in bulk, for example racks of servers, and sell access in smaller portions as individual virtual machines as needed by the consumer. For larger systems they operate them as multi-tenancy, where one installation is managed for multiple consumers using a small portion of the total system resources. This, I believe, is a much better concept to have in mind than a utility when engaging with the cloud.

The Cloud as a Service

As we saw in our earlier definition of cloud, it is common to refer to different segments of the cloud as a service: Infrastructure as a Service (IaaS), Platform as a Service (PaaS), and Software as a Service (SaaS). New types are also gaining traction, such as Function as a Service (FaaS) and Business Process as a Service (BPaaS). This is not a trivial observation. Let's look at what we mean by "as a Service," since it seems to be an important concept for the cloud.

In economics there is a fundamental distinction between goods and services. The precise distinction between the two remains disputed. In classical economics, the focus was on the goods as physical objects that had value, and over which one could have ownership rights. A good would be in the possession of the owner and could be bought and sold on a market.

Adam Smith in *The Wealth of Nations,* published in 1776, distinguished between two types of labor: productive and unproductive. Productive labor led to the production of tangible goods that could be stored and sold. This aided in the creation of wealth. Unproductive labor, however, did not produce any tangible goods but rather produced a service that perished at the time it was produced.

Today a service is considered something intangible that does not result in ownership. It is merely consumed by the buyer. Some definitions claim that a service does not have to do with anything physical, but that does not hold in all cases, as we saw with utilities. Water is indeed physical and can also be owned as a matter of fact. Goods, on the other hand, are physical and can be owned but can also be immaterial such as intellectual property rights. There is therefore still some overlap.

Because most of the services we see in the cloud are automated and do not directly depend on labor as classical services, we don't have to concern ourselves with classical economics' discussions of whether the labor is productive or not or weather it contributes to wealth. The key point about a service in the context of the cloud is that it is something that is not owned, but rather can be used. It is also intangible because it depends on software and data being communicated through a network.

The different kinds of services are essentially different packages of functionality offered to the consumer. Infrastructure as a Service (IaaS), for example, offers the functionality of infrastructure to the consumer. The provider handles everything to support the service. This is similar to a restaurant, which handles everything needed to provide the meal for consumption, like shopping, preparation, the room, and the furniture. The consumer of IaaS similarly doesn't own the infrastructure consumed (although data and code on that infrastructure can be owned, but that is different). The consumer still needs to do a lot of things with IaaS because it is just like renting a blank computer. The consumer has to install all the applications and configure it to perform the needed functions.

At the other end of the scale, we have Software as a Service (SaaS), where a neatly packaged product is offered to the consumer, who does not have to do anything in terms of managing, installing, or developing software. This is also something intangible, a service that is not owned by the consumer. It is a package of functionality but a qualitatively different one that implies a lot less responsibility on the part of the consumer in order to make it functional. It also implies a lot less flexibility in terms of functionality, since the service cannot be customized to the same degree. No special functions that are unique to the consumer can be supplied. The more you move from IaaS over PaaS to SaaS, the less responsibility you have as a customer, but you also have less flexibility. Consequently, you have to find the right level of service.

Think of it like going on vacation. Some people want maximum flexibility and just buy the tickets to the destination and then go out to explore. Maybe they already know the territory or have friends or they brought a tent or they reserved a hotel somewhere else. This is similar to IaaS. It definitely allows for flexibility but also requires responsibility and action.

Other people maybe buy a complete package with plane and hotel and transport from the airport to the hotel. They still have the flexibility to go and explore restaurants at the destination or rent a car and go for a trip somewhere. The travel agency handles only the travel and hotel the consumer the rest. This is similar to PaaS.

That last kind of traveler buys the all-inclusive package, where all the trips have been planned in advance and all meals are served at the destination hotel. The consumer is not responsible for anything and the traveler only has to animate the vacation with their good spirits and visit the pool or the beach or stay up all night singing Karaoke. It will not be possible to suddenly go bungee jumping or walk the Inca trail with this model. This is similar to SaaS.

The Cloud as Layers

In technology in general, the concept of layers is important. It is an abstraction that does not have any real physical basis but guides and encapsulates functionality in manageable bits. An example is the Open Systems Interconnection (OSI) model for communication between computer systems. It's used as a reference for communication over computer networks and therefore also the cloud. It consists of seven layers:

- Layer 1: Physical Layer—Transmission of raw streams of bits in a physical medium

- Layer 2: Data Link Layer—The connection between the two nodes

- Layer 3: Network Layer—Provides the functionality to transfer data sequences

- Layer 4: Transport Layer—Provides the functionality of controlling and maintaining the quality of a connection

- Layer 5: Session Layer—Controls the exchange of data in a session between two computers

- Layer 6: Presentation Layer—Provides a mapping between the application layer and the underlying layers

- Layer 7: Application Layer—The layer closest to the end user

In order for something to be transmitted, it has to go through the physical layer. There is no way around it. But it is inconvenient for the end user to be coding the message into strings of bits. Consequently, the different layers wrap a particular functional area of concern that can interface with the layers above and below it. There is no natural or physical reason it has to be like this, but in order to work productively this has proven helpful.

Layering allows for division of labor too. A web developer can focus only on the functions and commands offered at Layer 7 and has to know nothing about any of the other layers. The electrical engineer who is designing parts for a cellphone needs to know about Layers 1 and 2, while the engineer who is designing routing software needs to know about Layers 3 and 4.

In the cloud, which builds on these communication layers, the situation is similar, although there is no commonly shared standard similar to the OSI model that defines responsibilities and protocols for the different layers. A common way to look at it is the following. IT is often used in the context of explaining the cloud:

1. Network—Connection of the physical property to other networks and the internal network of the data center

2. Storage—The functionality necessary for storing data

3. Servers—Machines with a CPU that can to process data

4. Virtualization—A virtualization of the machine resources

5. Operating system—The operating system offered to higher level functionality

6. Middleware—Software that provides functionality to applications beyond those of the operating system

7. Runtime—The functionality to run a program

8. Data—Representation of binary information in a format readable by programs

9. Applications—The programs that define functionality

As you can see, this model is far from as neat and sequential as the OSI model. For example, why is Layer 8 (data) not on top of Layer 2 (storage)? And why is storage lower than the server? One would think that storage and data might be parallel. However, the purpose of the layering model is much the same as the OSI model: to delineate areas of responsibility and division of labor.

Again, an application programmer should only be concerned with the application layer. The operations professional would be concerned with Layers 6 and 7, and the infrastructure professionals with Layers 2 to 5. Network specialists would focus on Layer 1. Each of these groups is able to focus only on their area and disregard what goes on in the other layers. Operations specialists do not need to know anything about the application layer in order to do their job.

Such is the power of layering in cloud computing and it has allowed increased division of labor and specialization. The earliest programmers had to be masters of all layers in order to get any result. Now, thanks to the layering and partial standardization of the layers, it is possible to work independently of other surrounding layers. This becomes particularly important for the cloud since cloud providers assume responsibility and offer a layer as a service. This allows the consumers to choose at which level they want to take advantage of the cloud.

Because each layer is offered as a service, we can take advantage of the insight described here. Some are adventurous backpackers who want great flexibility and have the know how to manage lower levels. Others just want some sun and curacao drinks at the bar and opt for the higher levels when it comes to consumption. The right level depends on the context, which we return to later in the book. For now, it is important to understand the nature of the choice.

Summary

In this chapter we saw how an abstraction used for sketching technical solutions resulted in the cloud becoming the symbol for cloud computing. This symbol was taken up more widely and used for building new business models focused on the Internet. It was a conceived of as a marketing term that took a decade to catch on in the wider population. But once it did catch on, it quickly became a dominating concept.

The definitions of the cloud arose in a context where potential customers needed support to navigate the market to figure out what true cloud computing was. The NIST definition has come to delineate much of the vocabulary we use today around cloud computing, but certain aspects no longer fit perfectly with the cloud market.

We saw that a number of concepts were important in how we conceptualize the cloud. An old and persistent version had the cloud pitched as a utility. Closer inspection, however, revealed that this is a bit of a stretch. A better way to look at the cloud is as a form of retail.

The concept of the cloud as a service that stems from the earliest definitions continues to be important. Although it differs somewhat from a classical economical concept of a service, it does point to important aspects of the cloud—that it is based on consumption and does not entail ownership of the computing resources.

Finally, we saw how the concept of layering has aided the cloud in developing areas of specialization to support division of labor between different groups of specialists. By supplying layers as services, this has fueled development in the cloud where consumers can choose the level of flexibility/responsibility they want.

Why Cloud?

Now that we have a firmer grip on what the cloud is, it is easier to see why it is such a big deal. The cloud is transforming and will continue to transform the computing industry. In the future we may talk about on-premise data centers in the same way as we do about mainframes today, as relics of the past that definitely work well enough, but are mostly used because moving away from them entirely was too difficult. Some applications will probably remain in the on-premise data center as they have on the mainframe, but no one will build new data centers of their own unless they have very particular reasons. The cloud will be the default place to go. In this chapter, we look at why the cloud is the future. We see how the market is already moving fast toward the cloud and also look at the main drivers of cloud computing.

The Cloud Is the Future

Even companies that have the scale to run a competitive on-premise data center like Netflix have moved to the cloud. Some like Spotify, who could have started in the cloud, initially thought an on-premise data center was necessary but gave up and moved to the cloud. For many this is an emotional subject. One should not forget that the majority of the IT workforce see their area of expertise tied not to the cloud but to on-premise technologies and running a data center, a point we will return to in a later chapter.

The same was the case for the drivers of horse-drawn carriages who were taken over by the automobile. Many arguments could and were made in favor of the horse against the car. The danger of the automobile was one of them, which incidentally is also one of the major arguments against the cloud that

© Anders Lisdorf 2021
A. Lisdorf, *Cloud Computing Basics*,
https://doi.org/10.1007/978-1-4842-6921-3_2

we also return to in a later chapter. This was real enough. Early automobiles were dangerous but much of the danger was attributed to the fact that pedestrian behavior did not change with the advent of this new technology. The early days of the automobile saw the necessity for a shift in how to use the technology and how people adapted to it. It is a process and it is not finished yet.

It is, however, clear when we look at projections of cloud adoption that the cloud, like the automobile, is here to stay. A Gartner survey of IT leaders in 2019 revealed that the cloud comprised around 10% of total IT budgets. This means that the cloud is already mainstream but has a lot more opportunity to grow and this growth is fast. Gartner projects that the entire cloud market will grow to $355BN in 2022 from $197BN in 2018. The expected Compound Annual Growth Rate is 16% compared to 7% for traditional IT. The cloud is also in the top three areas where global CIOs will increase their spending.

If we look at the different segments in the cloud, the SaaS segment is the one with the fastest growth. It's projected to almost double in the five-year period from 2018 to 2022, from $86BN to $151BN, according to Gartner. The second highest growth is projected in the IaaS segment, from $32BN in 2018 to $74BN in 2022. Although these numbers are from before the COVID-19 pandemic, it has only exacerbated the need for the cloud and the speed of adoption is expected to increase.

Drivers for Cloud Adoption

To better understand the reasons for this shift, let's look at what drives adoption of the cloud. Because the cloud is a new type of technology it has to compete with existing alternatives. That alternative is to run an on-premise data center. That is similar to running your own generator compared to receiving your electricity from a utility company. There could be reasons for that for sure, but most organizations have little benefit from doing so. However, as we saw earlier, it is not as simple just to switch from your local data center to the cloud as it would be to switch from a local generator to a utility's power. It is much messier and therefore the drivers have to be stronger. Different organizations have different priorities, but most will have one of the following as a key driver for adopting the cloud over on-premise solutions.

Economy

It is evident that economic concerns are primary drivers of cloud adoption. This goes both for the provider and the consumer side of the equation. Both stand to gain from increased adoption of the cloud.

CAPEX to OPEX

A frequently mentioned sentence is that the cloud helps users move from CAPEX to OPEX. This means that costs are moved from capital expenditures (CAPEX), that is initial up-front investments, to operational expenditures (OPEX), or ongoing costs. When you buy a lot of equipment in order to support future demand of computing resources, a few things happen.

First of all, it ties up capital that could have been spent on other investments in the organization. This impacts the cash flow of a company. This is one of the key metrics that companies are measured on by investors and shareholders. The better the cash flow, the better the valuation of the company. The reason for this is not trivial. If a company runs out of cash and cannot pay its bills, it could result in bankruptcy, no matter how many servers they bought and no matter how promising the software on it is.

Another point is that a server is what is called a depreciating asset. That means it is something that loses its value over time. We are familiar with this dynamic in cars. The reason that private persons are opting to lease cars is the same reason that companies are opting for the cloud rather than investing in the hardware: we have little use for assets that we know will lose their value with time. This is not the same for all asset types. Real estate, for example, is not the same. It might appreciate and if it depreciates it will rarely go as fast or as low as servers. A server bought five years ago is virtually worthless and there is no big market for vintage computers.

Cost is more predictable in the cloud. There is typically some sort of monthly fee, although that can vary with consumption for some types of cloud services. But compare this to the old world of IT driven by capital investment. Projects are delayed all the time and budgeting is a yearly exercise, so no one knows if the money will be there next year. People in the IT industry will know the year end frenzy to spend this year's budget on something random that may or may not come in handy next year. Then come next year, the project may be cancelled altogether, and the investment proved to be wasted. This is a familiar dynamic.

Operational expenses are also easier to scale with changes in the market. If a company suddenly sees a downturn and loses revenue, a cloud model based on paying monthly fees based on consumption is easier to scale than a CAPEX model, where capital has been committed at the beginning of a multiyear period. In the cloud, the costs scale more easily up and down with the activity of the company.

A more subtle motivation for switching to an OPEX is that lower levels of capital investment will inevitably lead to lower levels of debt. And lower levels of debt in a company improve its credit rating, which means it is able to secure needed capital at a lower price. Consequently, investment in the cloud can be seen as part of a virtuous circle from an economic perspective.

Total Cost of Ownership

Although moving from CAPEX to OPEX is a win in itself for most private companies, it is not the same for all types of organizations. Governmental organizations work on a different set of premises than do private companies. The government is not concerned in the same way about cash flow or depreciating assets since they don't work by the logic of the balance sheet in the same way. Governmental organizations often have the reverse desire to bring down the commitments of the future and to pay for everything up front and not worry about it anymore. It has been common practice to allocate big capital budgets rather than operational budgets. The reasons are several, but a common one is that no political administration wants to be seen as having high levels of operational spending, as this is viewed by the public as unnecessary overhead. Investments, on the other hand, are better sold as visionary and meaningful. Unfortunately, this doesn't translate well to the cloud model of consumption.

Consequently, there has to be other economic reasons to invest in the cloud. One of them is total cost of ownership. Luckily it is indeed possible to bring down the operating expenses with the cloud, even compared to the traditional on-premise model. The reason is that, even though an IT asset, whether it is hardware or software, is paid for up front, buyers often also have to buy yearly support and an upgrade plan along with it. This is typically in the region of 10% to 20% of the initial purchase price. The price of many cloud services dwarf even that figure. I have been part of projects for public clients that saw reductions in operational costs by 80% to 90% without any capital expenditure—just by switching to the cloud.

Economies of Scale

The last economic driver is economies of scale and this applies to the supply side. The basic idea is that the cost of adding one unit of infrastructure decreases with the number of units already managed. This is a rule that also holds for other types of infrastructure like roads, telephone, gas, etc. The reasons are many, but to put it simply, let's look at the example of a startup. If they buy 10 servers, they need one full-time employee to manage those servers. The first 10 servers come with a cost of one full-time IT specialist. This person is difficult to recruit because they are already scarce in the market and the company may have to hire a recruiter, which brings additional costs. If something weird happens to the servers, the company may have to hire consultants to fix it.

Now compare this to AWS. If they buy 100 extra servers, it still would not require them to hire an extra IT specialist. They would also likely get a substantial wholesale discount. They definitely don't need a recruiter because people are lining up to work for them. If something weird happens to one of the servers, AWS likely already has an in-house specialist since the same weird thing happens much more frequently when you run thousands of servers and thus it makes sense to hire a specialist for this particular purpose.

Security

Although this is not the most common driver, it can be a powerful one. Many think of the cloud as insecure compared to on-premise, but recent advances in securing the cloud and changes in risk are changing that conception. If you have a data center that is completely cut off from the surrounding world you may feel like you have more control. But that is rarely if ever the case. Today's world is by definition connected. Employees may access the company system from home and the company has an Internet site. This leaves the complete system vulnerable for the ever-emerging new threats from around the globe.

Keeping Up with Threats

A company relying on its own data center needs to keep on top of all developing threats and attacks, 24/7. This is costly and difficult. A local IT security department needs to be staffed with specialists. In the cloud, some threats are easier to mitigate. Let's look at a couple of examples.

The classic distributed denial of service (DDoS) attack is where a number of machines controlled in a so-called bot network start sending multiple requests to a website. This can increase traffic 100 or 1000-fold, which very few websites are built to withstand. The effect is that it is taken offline and customers cannot place orders or get in contact with the company. In the cloud such attacks are easier to mitigate. There are systems that can detect infected machines and scale quite significantly to cope with the increased demand.

Keeping Information Safe

In terms of information security, recent legislation among others from the EU in the form of GDPR requires that companies are in much better control of personally identifiable information (PII). Cloud vendors now offer systems that will run reports and identify places where this information may be stored on internal resources and can also log who accessed the information when. There is also the possibility to automatically detect other vulnerabilities in the system configurations that would otherwise have taken an extensive audit to detect.

Encryption is now offered in the cloud by default, but is harder to set up on-premise. Encryption requires keys and they require adequate management for the system to be secure. Such systems are rarely in place on-premise but are easily available in the cloud and integrated into the services. Identity and Access Management (IAM), which makes sure that only authenticated and authorized users can access system resources and data, is built into the cloud by default, but has to be maintained in parallel on-premise.

As you can see, there are many reasons that security is a driver for the cloud. Vendors have a much better chance at keeping up with emerging threats and developing adequate ways of mitigating them.

Resilience

For most companies, business continuity is a key concern and because business operations are increasingly tied to IT, resilience becomes a key motivation. If an organization needs to make sure that its operations do not cease in the face of a natural or other disaster, they need to ensure the resilience of their IT operations.

The classical natural disasters like flooding, earthquake, hurricane, or volcanic eruption have the potential to completely destroy a data center. In order for this not to happen, a company has to build at least one backup site. This site needs to run exactly the same system setup as the primary one and there has to be automatic failover when the primary site fails. Not only is this expensive, it is also difficult to implement. To remain efficient, the company has to periodically conduct drills where the primary data center is shut down and the secondary center takes over. Many companies have such complicated setups that the drill in itself is far from a trivial risk.

In the cloud, this is in some cases virtually reduced to a few clicks that will give you even better geographical redundancy than was feasible for the company alone. Moreover, you can do this at the individual server level. If you want to make sure an earthquake in the U.S. West data center does not affect continuity, you can just chose to have it failover to a region in the U.S. East. No need to secure the connection and conduct drills. It is not even necessary to have the entire system running. It is possible to specify a template of the virtual machines that should spin up in the event of a server failure. This saves cost and energy for the company.

Another example of how the cloud can be used for resilience is for backups. It is not trivial to run a backup and recovery setup on-premise. Machines have to be added to the network and tested. In the cloud, storage for the backups is a fraction of on-premise costs and can be expanded with a few clicks. Consequently, some customers start with the cloud just for backups.

Scalability

Scalability is one of the most obvious benefits and one that is of particular importance for companies that grow quickly. We already learned that economically it required a lot of upfront payment to secure adequate system resources. But the cost is just one thing, the other is getting it fast enough and at the right locations to scale with demand. Especially in a global context, this can be a challenge.

Websites often see natural spikes in volume. Maybe the company has a sale, or it aired a successful commercial that generated a lot of interest. Maybe something went viral that prompted users to go to the website. Because website responsiveness is a key factor, it is necessary to be close to the customers geographically. For a small startup with global ambitions, it is not feasible to build up data center operations on all continents, but with content delivery networks this is again possible with just a few clicks. This is not just for companies. Cities may also want to make sure that a local disaster like a hurricane does not take down their website because residents want information. This can easily be scaled with the cloud.

Another example is how a traditional data center database administrator has to constantly monitor the storage available to a database and increase it or move it to a different server if it fills up. With cloud-based databases, that is no longer necessary. They will scale by themselves almost infinitely, depending on the particular service. It is also possible to scale up to hundreds of servers automatically if needed. This is why scalability is an important driver for many companies.

Focus

Because the cloud provider takes over much of the management of the IT infrastructure and because managing an IT infrastructure is not the business that most companies find themselves in, it can allow a company to focus its energy on its core competences. Today similarly, most companies don't want to build their own buildings, roads, and power stations, either because these are rarely aspects that provide a competitive advantage.

In business strategy, much attention is given to identifying and cultivating a company's competitive advantage. This is something that this company can and wants to do better than their competitors. For Apple, for example, this is the design of user-friendly products, not manufacturing the products. This is why Apple designs their products at its headquarters in California and outsources the production to another company, Foxconn in China, whose competitive advantage is not design, but manufacturing electronics products.

In much the same way that Apple doesn't have a competitive advantage in manufacturing their products, most companies do not have any competitive advantage in managing their own IT infrastructure. Using the cloud allows companies to focus on what they do best.

Agility

The importance of the ability to react fast to changing market conditions came into full view during the COVID-19 pandemic, where suddenly cloud solutions came even more into focus. With everyone in quarantine, the easiest way to work was in the cloud due to its universal access.

Elasticity means that consumption not only expands when necessary but also that it contracts when the need is gone again. Otherwise it would be necessary to keep paying for system resources that were no longer needed.

This dynamic is difficult to implement in an on-premise data center since you can't return the servers or the software licenses once you are done with them. Companies that see great spikes or uneven usage have a particular need for elasticity, since that allows them not to pay continuously for the peak load.

Another important part of agility is that system resources are available on demand when needed. If a particular database is needed, it shouldn't be necessary first to contact sales at the software company, get a quote, purchase it, and then install it. In the cloud all of this is reduced to searching for it on the cloud provider's website and then clicking it. Licenses are included in the metered usage of the service.

With this kind of usage, it is also easier to support innovation. If this was just an experiment, a proof of concept, it can be provisioned and used. Once it is no longer needed, it can be deleted and no further payments have to be made. This makes innovation and experimentation much cheaper.

Sustainability

A rarer but emerging driver is that the cloud is more sustainable when it comes to energy consumption. There are different reasons for that. First of all, a cloud provider may ensure a much better utilization of resources.

When you turn on a computer, its CPU runs no matter if it is used or not. Mostly CPUs idle and don't do anything. At a company where people work from 9 to 5, the computing resources will be used only in the time frame and typically not fully utilized at any point. That means that a traditional server running 24/7 is using three times as much energy as is needed. In the cloud, with elasticity and pooled resources, it is possible to secure a much better utilization since multiple customers can use the same machines. When utilization drops, machines will turn off and come back up again with increased use.

Another reason that the cloud is more sustainable is that it is easier to build efficient energy consumption into larger data centers. Energy for cooling can be reduced by up to 40%. Excess heat can be captured and turned into hot water. Because data centers also take up a considerable area of land, it is possible for them to set up solar cells to harvest energy. For example, Microsoft has vowed to be carbon negative by 2030, which means that they will produce more clean energy than they consume.

Summary

As we can see, investments in the cloud are already substantial and they are growing more than twice as fast as investment in other types of information technology. The market is converging toward the cloud as the default model. The reasons for this differ across different types of organizations.

Economically, the ability to shift from up-front commitment of capital to ongoing costs is attractive for private companies. The total cost of ownership will appeal to everyone, but is particularly valuable to public costumers seeking to lower their costs, while economies of scale ensures that cloud providers can continuously offer cloud services cheaper as the volume expands.

The cloud also allows for increased control of security and mitigation of risks. Due to the setup of modern cloud platforms, it is possible to increase the resilience of the IT infrastructure of any organization compared to an on-premise setup.

Scaling system resources is attractive and, along with the agility of cloud consumption, it makes it attractive for companies that have uneven utilization patterns or need for technological innovation.

The fact that a lot of capital is freed up and IT infrastructure work becomes obsolete allows companies to focus on their competitive advantage. Most companies do not have a need to run a data center and can therefore focus on their core competences by using the cloud.

A final emerging driver is sustainability, since professional cloud providers are much more likely to manage a data center that efficiently uses energy and may even supply it themselves with wind or solar power.

There are many drivers and different ones will appeal to different organizations, but even though the cloud is already mainstream, it still seems poised for further growth.

The Genealogy of Cloud Computing

It is important to understand the concept of the cloud and what it can be used for, but it is also important to understand the technical innovations that led to what we now call the cloud. The purpose of this chapter is to give an overview of the history of key components of the cloud in order to better understand why they were developed and how they shaped today's cloud computing landscape.

What we call the cloud today is a result of multiple different strands of technical developments. Many of these go far back in time and have surprising origins. Even if one is not historically inclined, it helps in understanding many of the contemporary features to know where they came from. Therefore, we will go through these different lines in the same fashion as a genealogy. We will trace relationships and see how key aspects developed historically.

© Anders Lisdorf 2021
A. Lisdorf, *Cloud Computing Basics*,
https://doi.org/10.1007/978-1-4842-6921-3_3

The first line refers to the development of the modern digital computer. The second has to do with the interfaces to this computer. The third relates how these computers are connected to form a network and the fourth digs into the software that forms the basis of modern cloud computing. This is not a comprehensive technical review, but it aims to highlight key aspects and developments.

Origin of the Computer

To compute means to calculate something and a computer is someone or something that does that calculation. Humans have used machines to help them calculate for thousands of years. As early as the 3rd millenium BCE, what is today known as the abacus existed. This is one of the oldest known computing tools. It is entirely mechanical and uses a system of beads on strings to represent numbers. It can be used for multiplication, addition, and other arithmetical functions.

Computing Machines

While the abacus is an example of a simple manual tool, other more complex machines were developed for calculation. One of the most impressive and perhaps earliest known analog computers is the Antikythera mechanism. It was found in an ancient Roman shipwreck in 1901, off the coast of the Greek Island of Antikythera, hence the name. It is traditionally dated to the first or second century BCE. It was composed of more than 30 gears and was able to calculate the position at different times of the moon, sun, eclipses, and lunar phases. It is the earliest known example of a computer of that complexity. It is even thought to have calculated the elliptical orbit of the moon. Knowledge that the moon and other planets had elliptical orbits was subsequently forgotten, only to be rediscovered by Johannes Kepler almost two millennia later in the 17th Century. The technical sophistication with which it was built was similarly forgotten until the 17th Century, when a couple of people invented machines that could calculate. Among them were the French mathematician Blaise Pascal and, improving on Pascal's design, Johan Gotfried Leibniz.

The Binary Paradigm

Leibniz was a contemporary and an intellectual match of Sir Isaac Newton, a genius who invented calculus in cooperation/competition with Newton and a pillar of modern mathematics. He is also in a sense the father of the idea of the modern computer, as he was the first to contemplate a binary computer-a machine that could calculate based on ones and zeros. This was before electricity had been tamed, so any practical application was mechanical and severely limited.

With the binary approach to computing, it was possible to create general purpose solutions. All the previous computing machines had been for specific purposes, like calculating the position of planets, addition, and multiplication. Building on a binary approach, it was possible to go beyond that.

It wasn't until Charles Babbage in the 1830s that a more comprehensive machine was designed that could benefit from this knowledge. His analytical engine was, however, never built and would only become feasible later, when electricity was properly harnessed.

Digital vs. Analog

The first truly binary machine was not a computer but a communication device, namely the telegraph popularized by Samuel Morse, who built it on earlier works of others. The advent of electricity made it possible to send discrete pulses through wire, which could be registered by an electromagnet at the other end.

Until the telegraph, all previous machines had been analog. With the telegraph we entered the "digital" era. The word digital was not used until a 100 years later. It was invented during World War II by another pioneer of computing, George Stibitz of Bell Telephone Laboratories. It was a replacement of the term "pulse" and meant that computing was done by electrical rather than mechanical means.

Tubes, Transistors, and Integrated Circuits

The first digital computers were built with vacuum tubes. They were convenient because they implemented binary logic and Boolean functions with electricity. The first such digital computer was the Z3, by the German Konrad Zuse during World War II, but it was destroyed during the war. A replica was built in 1961. Zuse originally built the Z1 as a mechanical computer in the mid-1930s unrelated to earlier research, which he only later became familiar with. He switched to radio tubes and built a prototype, the Z2, to secure funding for the Z3, which became operational in the 1940s.

The use of vacuum tubes for the digital computer resulted in machines that would take up the space of an entire room. This was the case with the ENIAC, built at the University of Pennsylvania in 1945. It was the first electric general-purpose computer that was Turing complete, which is a measure of what it means to be a computer. This eventually led to the commercial mainframe in the shape of the UNIVAC in 1951.

With the invention of semiconductors, which were smaller, more efficient, and durable, it became possible to make a smaller digital computer. The first mainframes were built with vacuum tubes but moved to semiconductors.

With integrated circuits, it was possible to build even smaller computers. This was used in the so-called minicomputer in the mid-1960s, which was smaller and cheaper to buy than a complete mainframe. This allowed research institutions to purchase them. While the mainframe was always a product for a select few companies, the minicomputer was produced by around 100 different companies. The minicomputer, with its wider appeal and usage, was instrumental in developing many of the core technologies and approaches of modern computing and cloud computing, for example in the area of operating systems, as you will see.

The Microprocessor

The microprocessor was a game-changer in computing, with its appearance in the early 1970s. This was essentially a computer on a chip and allowed computers to shrink even further in size and initiate a trajectory toward ever faster speeds of processing. With the microprocessor, it became feasible to build computers for personal use. This meant the birth of the personal computer. Without it we wouldn't have the PC, the Apple computer today, or the Commodores, Amstrads, and Ataris that some of us can remember from our childhood and youth. The personal computer is the primary medium used to access the cloud today.

The microprocessor also meant that powerful machines, called servers, could be developed. They were put in racks and used in data centers for enterprise purposes. The microprocessor was also the core of the web servers that powered the early commercial Internet and still are today.

The most lasting effect is that with the PC, computing became something everybody could engage in and this sped up innovation. While early hobbyists like Steve Wozniak were more interested in building the hardware, the egalitarian and sharing spirit of early pioneers developed into open source, where developers worldwide would contribute for free and develop software anyone could use. This has also had a tremendous impact on the cloud, as you shall see.

The Origin of Interfaces

Having a computer was only half the solution. The other half was how to interface with it. The earliest analog computers were comparatively simple since the area of function was constrained to a special purpose. In this case the interface reflected that special purpose. For a general-purpose computer built on binary codes, this becomes a more complex and pressing concern. The problem was how to control what the computer does.

Punch Cards to Terminals

In order to understand this development, we have to go back to the beginning of the 19th Century. Joseph Marie Jacquard was from a family of weavers and developed a system were looms were able to weave patterns based on cards with punched holes. The loom would use these cards to direct its weaving. This is the first example of mechanical control of a process but also of external memory since the cards were just that: memory.

This was a precursor, even if the details of how are not known, to American inventor Herman Hollerith's contribution. He developed a method that could store information about the 1890 U.S. census coded in cards with punched holes. Based on this method, Hollerith invented machines that could count and process information.

Using punch cards became the method of choice for interfacing with the digital computer. An operator would feed the cards, which had been punched (coded) by the programmer, into the computer. The first line of mainframes worked like this. This is also the origin of the term *batch processing,* since such a job would consist of serving a batch of cards into the computer.

The Teletype was developed in the 1960s for minicomputers. It had a standard keyboard with a few extra characters, most notably the @ that we all know as a part of an email address today. The keyboard thus became the standard way of interfacing with a computer.

Timesharing and the Client/Server Paradigm

It quickly became inconvenient for a single operator to take an entire batch and then switch to the next. It became more common to use terminals to access the mainframe and with this, the possibility of timesharing arose. The idea was that the operator feeding the cards would no longer be needed, instead the programmer could feed the code directly into the computer through a terminal and share the computing time with others connected to it.

This proved to be a powerful idea: you no longer had to be physically at the mainframe handing the cards to the operator. You could enter data from a much simpler machine. This is also the origin of the client/server paradigm. The idea is that a central entity, the server, performs the bulk of the computing, while the client is only used as an interface to pass information to and from the server. This means that the client does not have to perform everything locally and by extension. You did not need a mainframe in the room in order to use the mainframe.

This proved to have fundamental consequences for the cloud and is the basic premise of all cloud computing. The fact that you don't have to perform the computing and storage locally on your device is a key characteristic of the cloud. The way browsers and email work is according to this model. The browser simply sends instructions and receives results. It does very little computing itself.

Remote Connections

The client/server model led to the development of a standardized protocol called Telnet, which is still in use today. Introduced in 1969, Telnet is short for Teletype network and was a virtual implementation of the Teletype. This protocol makes it possible to access a computer anywhere on a network. Telnet provided a command-line interface to the remote computer, which involved interfacing via a window with text in crude characters. This is still a standard way that many programmers interface with the cloud. For some cloud vendors, it is the only way they interface.

The Telnet protocol, however, was not encrypted and thus it was vulnerable to wiretapping. This is why a new standard had to be developed. This was the Secure Shell (SSH) protocol, which was an encrypted way of connecting to a remote computer using a client/server model. On the computer to which access was needed, a server needed to be installed. On the accessing computer that would connect, send, and receive instructions, a client had to be installed. Today this is still the most widespread way of accessing virtual machines in the cloud across every cloud vendor.

Another way of making remote connections that's worthy of mention is the Remote Desktop Connection. This was built into the Windows operating system. It follows a protocol called RDP and allows you to basically look into another computer the same way as you would your own local computer. There are other versions of the same principle based on virtualization software in the market now, but the basic idea comes from the Remote Desktop Connection.

The Origin of Communication

Toward the end of the 60s, it became clear that computers could also be a powerful way to communicate. Not only would it be convenient to log in to a computer from far away, but having computers communicate and send data between them had great promise. Therefore, the race was on to provide the means for this communication. While we have grown accustomed to using the telephones to connect to the Internet, this was actually not a model that worked. Telephone lines at that time were analog and worked through circuit switching, that is, operators had to connect one call physically to the receiver. This model did not lend itself well to the digital communication needed by computers.

The idea for a network of computers exchanging data freely is usually attributed to the American computer scientist and psychologist J.C.R. Licklider. In a 1963 memo, he used the term *Intergalactic Computer Network* to describe the ideas he had in mind for a network of computers.

ARPANET and TCP/IP

Licklider was working at the U.S. Defense Department's Advanced Research Projects Agency, where he convinced others that this network was important. The primary concern at the height of the cold war was the threat of nuclear annihilation. The network Licklider had in mind would remain functional even if a few of the computers on the network were destroyed.

This was the start of the creation of ARPANET, an American defense project that linked computers together in a proto-Internet. Two key issues had to be solved in order to have a network where information would automatically flow between computers. The first was that a computer or any other node on the network needed to have an address and be able to exchange information in discrete packets with other addresses. This was solved with the Internet Protocol (IP), which has given us the term "IP address," still the core of all Internet and cloud communication today.

Another task was to be able to control the communication sent between two computers on the network. It was important to make sure that all data sent in a packet was received before the next packet was sent. This is what the Transmission Control Protocol (TCP) allowed computers to do, regardless of the content of the data. The TCP/IP protocol was thus developed for ARPANET, but became the foundation of communication on the Internet. It underpins all communication in the cloud today.

World Wide Web

It's one thing to have computers send small packets of data that is incomprehensible and yet another to have a higher layer that humans can use to communicate through computers. This is where the World Wide Web (WWW) comes into the picture. Tim Berners-Lee was a British researcher working at the European Organization for Nuclear Research (CERN) in Geneva, Switzerland. The initial idea came from a project that proposed a method for researchers to easily share and update information between them. By the end of the 1980s, CERN was the largest node on the Internet in Europe and Berners-Lee had the idea to join them to form a World Wide Web. He published the first website in December, 1991. The World Wide Web builds on three key elements: URL, HTTP, and HTML.

URL is short for Uniform Resource Locator. While the IP address is itself a unique location of a resource, it is inconvenient to remember and communicate a ten-digit decimal number. Instead, the URL or web address uses syntax to describe how to locate not only the node that holds the web page, but also where on the node the document is. This made it possible to structure a web domain into sub-domains accessible through the URL. This gave the increased flexibility of being able to precisely locate text on another computer without first connecting to the computer and then going through a search function to find the right page in the directory of the computer.

A URL is composed of a domain type (.com) that routes the traffic to a particular domain of that type (lisdorf.com) and if nothing more is given then the homepage is displayed. If you already know you want to go to a particular subpage, this can also be specified (lisdorf.com/blog).

The Hypertext Transfer Protocol (HTTP) transmits information between computers. Again, this is handled at a lower level by the TCP protocol, but this would also be very complex to write individual small packages of data and send to other computers. Rather, HTTP translates this from a higher-level language that humans can more easily understand into the lower-level that computers understand. It is built on a simple request-response model, where a request message is sent. A short list of commands is included in the specification, like GET, POST, and DELETE. This allowed a person to retrieve and modify a document on another computer on the network.

This document had to be written in HTML (Hypertext Markup Language). This format is based on markups, or codes, that determine how to display the document to users. A web browser interprets these codes and displays the document to the human end user. HTML has a variety of building blocks like images, text, and links to other documents. It may be seen that this was focused on research and text, but it has proved flexible. It's been able to adapt new elements such as interactive blocks, media, and payment methods, even if it wasn't designed for it. HTML is still the basis of everything we see on web pages in the cloud today.

The Origin of Software

The computer, its interfaces, and communication are all nothing without the software. As you learned, the modern computer was built with general-purpose computing in mind. The software allows special purposes to develop out of the general-machine properties of the computer. The most foundational software program is the operating system.

Operating Systems

In the early days of the computer, every program had to be compiled and run together with its input data. Compiling a program means translating the instructions of the program into machine code. For example, can a program calculate the trajectories of projectiles? Could one input the parameters, such as weight, force, and such into the program, which would yield the output (if it didn't fail, which it often did)?

Every new program necessitated resetting the computer and restarting it with a new program and its input. Many of the same variables had to be defined for each program. such as how to use memory, printing the results, and the like. This was repetitive and since everything was on cards, a library of cards was included with the purchase of a mainframe for these peripheral functions. Today, we would call them drivers. This library of common functions that programs could use was the precursor to the operating system. Today, libraries are still widely used in programming to create lists of common functions that can be called by a program, instead of having to write them every time.

An operating system is therefore a piece of software that provides a set of functions that programs can use. The first operating system was developed by GM for an IBM mainframe in 1956. The next problem was that operating systems were not, as we have become accustomed to today, similar across machines. They were tailored to the individual machine or range of machines. It was not until 1960 that IBM made the leap to develop one operating system for all its machines (OS/360), which at the time was a major undertaking, since computers differed widely. Some, for example, had more memory than others and adequate functioning had to be ensured across the full range of specifications.

At the same time, AT&T Bell Labs was developing an operating system for the minicomputer toward the end of the 1960s. It was called UNIX and was free. It was written in the programming language C, which made it portable to any computer that could compile a program in C, which was a pretty standard feature for mincomputers at the time. The minicomputer had a wider user group, especially in the research world, so this made it widespread and fueled a lot of innovation. For example, the University of California, Berkeley developed the Berkeley Software Distribution (BSD), which is the ancestor of most modern open source operating systems as well as macOS X, which runs on Apple computers.

Perhaps the biggest impact was the inspiration for another open source project for computers based on the microprocessor, called Linux. It was initially developed in the early 1990s and became standard across many vendors, who offered their own flavor of it. However, it was another operating system for the personal computer that gained an early lead and for decades and was the de facto standard for microprocessor-based computers. That was called DOS (Disk Operating System).

A small company of young and geekish looking men were tasked with supplying the operating system for IBM's new personal computer. The company was to become one of the behemoths of the cloud and was called Microsoft. Their solution, DOS, allowed users to type commands to load and start programs for example. This was done in the traditional console type of interface with a black screen and simple text. With the success of the PC, DOS became widespread.

It wasn't until the release of the successor, called Windows in 1985, that the operating system got a human friendly interface with windows that contained different programs running on the machine. The MacIntosh was, however, the first to introduce that functionality. But since they were tied to the machines made by Apple and not available to other hardware producers, the Windows operating system in its successive versions became the de facto standard for the personal computer and for most servers that powered data centers.

This was the picture for a couple of decades, until the open source community managed to produce a functionally equivalent in Linux, which was free. This became the basic operating system for the early cloud pioneer Amazon and has stayed with the cloud since then. Today, even Microsoft runs as many Linux servers as they do Windows servers.

Virtualization

Operating systems run on the machine in front of you and the cloud requires access to on-demand computing resources, which means you need to be able to access machines that are not in front of you. As you learned earlier, the SSH and RDP protocols allow users to access a machine through a network, but that is still just one machine that has to be set up, plugged in, and configured. This is why virtualization was developed. This allowed multiple "virtual" computers to run on one machine or to be moved to another machine, thus making the operating system independent not only of the type of machine but of any particular machine.

This model has been used extensively in on-premise data centers, but is even more of a game changer in the cloud. Suddenly anyone could get access to an operating system that provided the computing resources needed over the Internet in a matter of minutes, without having to buy and install a machine. The OS could be accessed the same way as the internal virtual machines, that is, through RDP or SSH.

Containers

Having access to an operating system is a great convenience, but often you'll write programs that only use a fraction of the functionality of an operating system and, after all, you just want to run your program. This is where so-called containers come into play. A container is a further abstraction on top of an operating system that can be packaged and moved around, even across cloud providers. They can be spun up according to predefined specifications very quickly and retired just as quickly. They are not only popular ways to deploy programs in the cloud, but are also used behind the scenes for many of the functionalities that cloud providers supply.

An example of this is the ability to write code that is executed without a need to deploy any program. This is the ultimate abstraction, where in principle just the code could move around to different cloud vendors based on price or preference. This is sometimes called Function as a Service (FaaS), since it allows the provider to offer a service where the consumer only needs to write the function. All other aspects of the infrastructure are handled by the provider.

A new paradigm raises the abstraction to a level where you don't even have to write the code anymore. This is the so-called "no code" paradigm, where functions are offered, and the user simply has to configure them.

As can be seen, the movement has been one of successive levels of abstraction. First the machine was abstracted from the operating system, then the operating system was abstracted from the particular type of machine, then the operating system was abstracted across machines, leading to applications being abstracted from the operating system in containers, and finally the code being abstracted from the application or even code abstracted altogether.

Databases

While the operating system is for general-purpose computing and allows users to run any type of program on it, there are also other types of more specialized software that are important to understand. Since much of modern computing concerns access to and manipulation of data, the development of dedicated system for handling this was a key concern. The mainframes and minicomputers all had memory and were able to access this through different versions of filesystems. It was difficult to manipulate and quickly scan the data in these files and consequently necessary to run a program that looked through all the files if a particular datapoint was needed.

This is why the database was invented as a specialized software component for storing and retrieving data. While the ideas behind the relational database initially described in formal mathematical terms by E.F. Codd in 1970 proved to be transformative, it is important to remember that the relational model was not the first or only type of database developed. It did become almost synonymous with database from the 1980s onward. One of the major cloud platforms, Oracle, grew out of the relational database technology.

With the advent of the Internet and different ways of programming, there was a revival of different new types of databases. They are in many cases built specifically for the cloud and the types of programming problems the Internet offers. Many of these have been open sourced and offered as similar services across the different vendors. The database market is one of the biggest in the cloud today.

The database is a platform that can be used for a particular purpose, in this case data storage and access. Following the lead of the database, other platforms have evolved to define the so-called platform as a service (PaaS) model. Examples include messaging, application development, and integration.

Business Software

An important development in software was standardized or Commercial Off the Shelves (COTS) software. These are programs that can be installed on any computer running the operating system they were programmed for. Before this became standard, a company needed to hire software developers to write custom applications for any business functions. Initially so-called Materials Resource Planning (MRP) were popular at factories that needed to figure out how much was needed of different materials in order to sustain production and not waste a lot of money on excess stock.

This developed into the so-called Enterprise Resource Planning (ERP) software that was conceived more broadly. An early pioneer was the German company SAP. Rather than offering a custom developed program, they offered a standard program that could be configured and customized when needed. A key innovation of SAP's R/3 was to build the software in functional modules that could be bought separately but would work together if needed. Such modules supported a complete business function. This was the innovation championed by SAP. Examples include financial accounting, controlling, materials management, and human resources. A company was then able to piece together an ERP solution made up of the modules that they needed, rather than build one comprehensive custom system that did everything.

This approach has become the standard. Other pioneers like PeopleSoft and Siebel focused more narrowly on HR and CRM, but still kept the modular approach. This has paved the way for modern Software as a Service (SaaS), which is typically even more focused on one or a few particular business functions like payroll, customer service, talent management, etc.

Summary

This chapter discussed a selection of technical developments that together form the basis of modern cloud computing. Cloud computing depends on four parallel lines of development that frequently interact (see Figure 3-1).

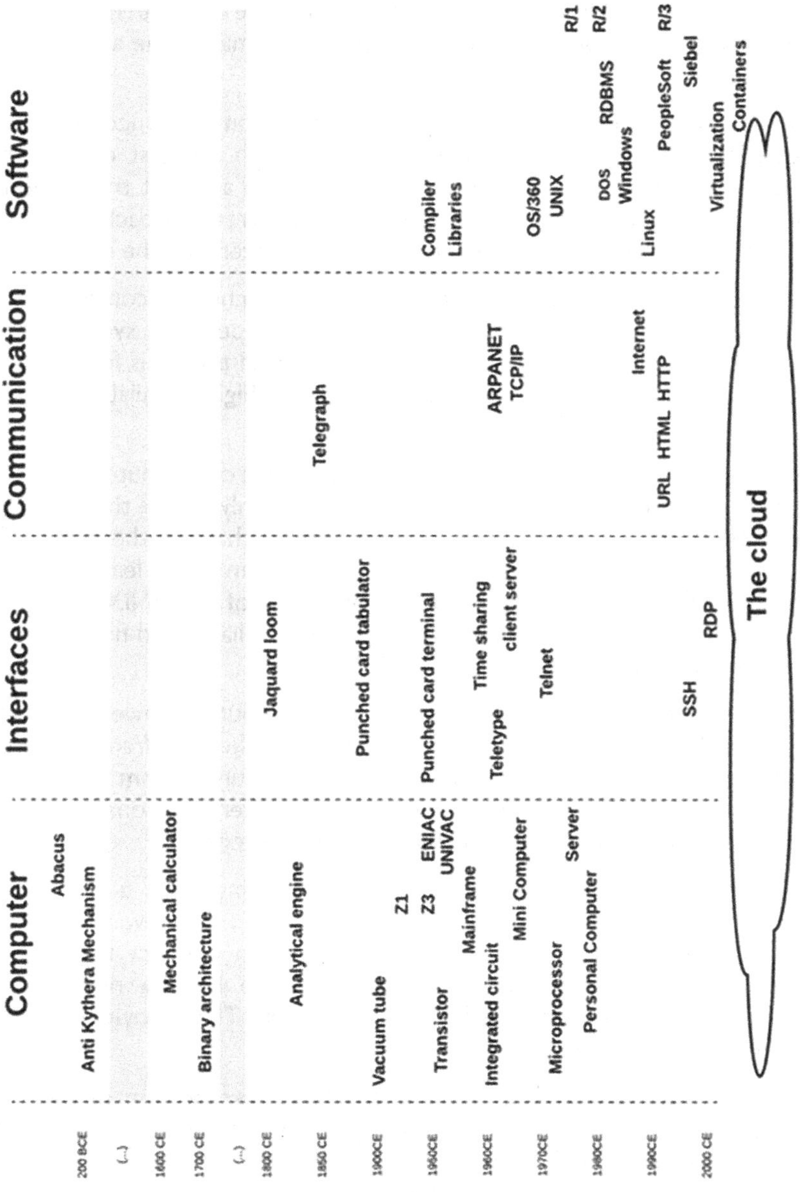

Figure 3-1. The genealogy of the cloud

The primary line is the *computer*, where the idea of a binary general-purpose machine gradually overtook the mechanical, special-purpose machines. With the invention of the vacuum tube, it became feasible to leave the analog mechanical approach and build computers based on electromechanical binary functions. This led to the first mainframe computers. The subsequent invention of the semiconductor made it possible to shrink the mainframe and make it more reliable.

The first way to interface with the machine came from the success of the punch card and this became the way to interact with the first computers. With the success of the mainframe came the need to abstract the different machines, so developers did not have to redo the program for each individual machine. This led to the invention of the operating system for the mainframe.

The integrated circuit allowed for an even smaller and cheaper computer, the minicomputer, which similarly had a need for an operating system. This became the UNIX operating system, which has formed the basis for much of modern computing. It spread more widely due to the higher availability of the minicomputer and it being free.

With the invention of the microprocessor, another type of computer emerged that would become critical for the cloud. Not only does the PC use microprocessors to access the cloud, but the servers that run the cloud also run on microprocessors. While Windows became an early leader in the personal computing space, it was Linux that grew out of the UNIX operating system. It came to overtake the server side, being a reliable and flexible, free open source alternative.

It was early realized that physical proximity to a computer allowed only one person to work at a . The idea of time sharing on the mainframe allowed multiple people to work on the same computing resources from a distance. This formed the client/server pattern, with much weaker functionality on the client side and strong computing capability on the server side.

The keyboard became the default way of interfacing with a computer, overtaking the punch cards. Protocols were developed to allow a keyboard interface (or in effect any programming interface) to connect to another computer. A natural continuation was therefore to build a network of computers, which was what ARPANET achieved. This provided a key foundation for the Internet.

In parallel, the World Wide Web was conceived as a way for humans to share information through text-based web pages on the Internet. This eventually provided the possibility for the cloud to develop outside the army and research context. Offering these basic computing services through the cloud would form the category of Infrastructure as a Service (IaaS).

Another parallel evolution was in writing discrete software modules that could be used by different programs like databases. These were eventually made available through the cloud and formed the category of Platform as a Service (PaaS), where more databases and similar components used by applications became available.

Enterprise software became standardized because it was costly for companies to each develop their own Enterprise Resource Planning applications. These applications offered a modular setup with individual applications that were built to work together but could be bought and operated separately. A business function could have its own standardized software module. This became the basis for the last major category of the cloud: Software as a Service (SaaS).

IBM

IBM (International Business Machines Corporation) is one of the most illustrious companies in the tech industry. In many ways, an argument could be made that IBM *created* the computer industry and many of the standards that go with it. If one were to point to one company as critical to the creation of modern computing, IBM would be a serious contender. Even more astounding is the fact that it has a history of more than 100 years, which predates the age of the computer! In this chapter, we look at how IBM's history has determined its culture and how it has influenced their approach to the cloud. Based on these insights, it is possible to understand what kind of company IBM is and how they approach the cloud.

The History of IBM

IBM's history predates not only cloud computing but computing in general. It all started in 1911 with a company called CTR, which was short for Computing – Tabulating – Recording. This company was formed out of three other companies that merged into a common entity.

© Anders Lisdorf 2021
A. Lisdorf, *Cloud Computing Basics*,
https://doi.org/10.1007/978-1-4842-6921-3_4

Building Business Machines

In order to understand the circumstances under which the company was formed, we need to think about the era in which this happened. First, it is important to remember that this was the time of the inventor and entrepreneur, sometimes embodied in the same person, as was the case with Thomas Edison. Commonly, the inventor was someone dabbling with a machine of some sort and a gifted entrepreneur understood how to market that machine. This is the model embodied by all three companies that came to make up CTR.

Second, at the end of the 19th Century, the financial markets were taking off and getting a lot of attention from investors of all sorts. It had become easier to buy and sell stock. It became common to buy a number of companies in the same business area and merge them into a trust and then float them on the stock market at a price above the combined market capitalization. The thinking was that, due to synergies and economies of scale, they would be worth more.

Charles Flint was one of these imaginative financiers. He created many interesting companies of this sort. For example, he created the United States Rubber Company, which quickly came to dominate its market. This was before the current regulations were in place. Flint imagined something similar could be done with what became CTR.

The first company he bought was the Bundy Manufacturing Company from Binghamton, New York, which came to be known as International Time Recording. Their product was a device to record when employees arrived at work and when they left. This system was used for more than a century at factories, and it is the origin of the term to "punch in."

The second company was the Computing Scale Company out of Dayton, Ohio. They supplied tabletop scales that allowed clerks to quickly calculate the price of goods.

The third and last company was also the one that came to be most famous, even though it did not dominate sales or focus initially in the newly formed company. It was Herman Hollerith's company, which came to be known as the Tabulating Machine Company. Hollerith had invented a system for using punch cards to represent data and tabulate it. The machine was much faster at aggregating and counting based on inputs from cards than when done with manual labor. The background was the U.S. census. In 1880, the census had tracked five different variables, but congress wanted to track more. Due to the increasing size of the American population, it had taken eight years to finish the report. Hollerith was a bright young engineer who had heard about using punch cards in relation to weaving. Based on this, he invented his tabulating machine. He secured the first patents in 1884 and soon after started selling the machines.

One thing that CTR took from the Tabulating Machine Company was its business model, which was based on leasing the machines to the customers and having them buy the cards. This was a lucrative business and the simple cardboard cards made up 5-10% of the company's revenue.

These three companies had a relatively clear idea behind them, focusing on the use of machines to help in computing and data processing. But they were geographically far from each other and their customer bases were different. In order to bring all these things together, Flint hired Thomas Watson Sr. in 1914. He came from National Cash Registers (NCR), which at the time was one of the most visionary companies, supplying managers to many other companies. NCR was one of the first producers of cash registers and built an impressive salesforce. Much of what Watson brought to IBM came from there. He focused the company on sales and technological innovation and brought the salespeople, who were out with customers, together with the engineers and the factory workers to make sure that innovation could take advantage of customer needs and production capabilities.

Watson wanted his salesforce to build a lasting relationship with customers and to gradually sell more solutions. This was underpinned by a specific reward structure, where the salesperson's quota was determined not on what they sold as such, but on the total value of the customer. If a customer bought something new but cancelled other products, the total value might decline and there would be no bonus. IBM's machines were expensive and only companies with a large volume of data processing were buying them. That meant that though IBM had just a few hundred customers, those customers were among the biggest companies and government agencies.

Up through the 1920s, CTR slowly consolidated their position and bought competitors in order to control patents. This was an early focus that landed them in anti-trust cases. The focus on innovations was also aimed toward securing patents, many of which never resulted in new features or products. It also had the effect of delaying the innovations' implementation in products since the patents had to be secured before the company was willing to market them. Still, a steady stream of innovations was marketed up through the 1930s. This secured a dominant market position of around 80-90%. At the same time, the international business grew and subsidiaries were opened all around the world. This led to the rebranding of the company to International Business Machines, which was a good description of what it did.

The focus of the company under Watson had been to empower customers with the use of machines. He said to new salespeople: "We are furnishing business men with highly efficient machines which save them money" and the overall goal of the company was "To serve better industry's vital requirements – the need to conserve time, motions, and money."

A consequence of how IBM operated was that machines were set up on location at the customer's site. These rooms were sometimes known as IBM rooms and were the same rooms in which mainframes were later set up. Thus, IBM was driving the creation of the data centers even before the invention of the computer. They were also driving the outsourcing model, since they provided IBMs as a service to smaller customers who could not afford to rent their own machines.

The Beginnings of the Computer

Thomas Watson Jr., who was Thomas Watson Sr.'s son, was among the first at IBM to see the potential of the computer, which he did so by the end of the 1930s. IBM had a keen focus on being able to recruit the best people from top universities and already had good ties with Columbia. At the time, IBM was trying to build a close relationship with Harvard as well. Howard Aiken, a Harvard physicist, was trying to build an electro-mechanical computing engine based on the ideas of Charles Babbage, but he couldn't secure funding from the university. IBM offered to work with Aiken and sponsor the development of the machine. The collaboration resulted in the Mark I, which was built by IBM and sent to Harvard in the beginning of the 40s. It is rumored that Harvard snubbed Thomas Watson Sr. at the time of presentation by "forgetting" to pick him up from the station and not mentioning IBM in the press release. This infuriated Watson Sr. and prompted IBM to enter the computing market with determination.

Although IBM was heavily involved in World War II on most other fronts, their electronic division was not engaged in the war effort and had time to work on a spinoff of the Mark I project. This turned out to be the 603 calculator and its successor, the 604. This was much smaller than other machines and could also calculate. It sold well and ushered in the time of electronic computing for IBM. They subsequently worked with University of Pennsylvania on the ENIAC computer, which was among the first computers in the world, but just as a parts supplier. Unlike many other technology companies, IBM was not involved in any government projects related to the computer. They had to recruit from universities and the army following the war in order to ramp up their efforts in the computing space.

IBM was thus not an initial leader in the computing industry. Indeed the UNIVAC, which grew out of the work with the ENIAC at the University of Pennsylvania, was an early leader in the computing market. It was eventually snatched up by Remington Rand, one of IBM's big competitors. IBM though had two advantages. First, they had established a new research center in Poughkeepsie, which cultivated a collaborative nature that fostered innovation. Second, they had already cultivated a close relationship with their customers and were able to work with them to provide them with what they needed.

Other early computer manufacturers came from the science and government space, but IBM already had deep relationships with most major companies through their tabulating equipment business.

IBM also had an understanding of working with universities and donated around a 100 computers to universities in order to get them to teach students programming. During the 1950s, IBM began steadily to dominate the computer market. A milestone was IBM's work with MIT and the U.S. Army to develop the SAGE system, which was the first geographically distributed real-time computing system spanning 23 different computers across America.

Increased investments in R&D led to the first transistor-based computer in 1960 and increased market share, but it was the development of the S/360 that secured IBM's dominance. The S/360 mainframe was more than just a computer. It was a line of computers. It was the first to have the same operating system across six different machines. This meant that programs could easily be moved to new and bigger machines if customers needed to upgrade. This product line established IBM as the undisputed computing company on the planet, with 80-90% of the market worldwide. Due to settlements in a long-running antitrust case, it became possible for others to write software for the IBM mainframe and supply peripherals.

The Commoditization of Computing and the Downfall of IBM

With the advent of the integrated circuit, the minicomputer gained in popularity due to its lower size and cheaper price. There has been much discussion about whether IBM missed that market, but in effect they also became dominant with the AS/400 as the best selling minicomputer of all. However, IBM never came close to the same monopoly as they had with the mainframe. The profit was not the same either. Eventually IBM developed the next computing revolution in the shape of the personal computer. This laid the foundation for another well known vendor in the cloud computing space: Microsoft.

From the 60s onward, most every computing organization and standards group had at least one representative from IBM. Not only did they foster innovation, they also drove its diffusion to other companies, customers, and government. This was the case with the relational database that benefitted another of the big cloud computing vendors, Oracle.

The Switch to Services, Software, and Hosting

Unfortunately, the success of IBM was predicated on continuous growth. When the market started changing, they were not able to change with it. IBM had a strong company culture from its very beginning, where employees were expected to be IBM for life. This meant that IBM would rather reappropriate talent than fire them. This became a problem by the end of the 70s and 80s, when margins were diminishing. Computing was becoming commoditized and customers' demands were shifting. This meant that IBM started having deficits.

This resulted in a redefinition of IBM from a product company to a service and software company. IBM had always been a sales-focused company and sales was the only way to the CEO slot. Even though R&D was an important focus area of IBM, no engineer could hope to serve as CEO. This meant that IBM would turn its focus on what it was best at: servicing its customers to get what they needed in terms of computing. Few companies in the world were more ubiquitous or had a better connection to its customers.

The service branch became the primary way that IBM reinvented itself. Through professional services, they helped their customers integrate their systems.

While IBM never shied away from buying hardware competitors, it started to buy software companies in the mid-90s to enter this market. Although IBM had many different software products, this was never a major source of revenue. This can be attributed to the fact that IBM only sold software for its own hardware, which was the mainframe. But when hardware profitability and sales volume in general and mainframe in particular started to drop, IBM had to look elsewhere for revenue. IBM realized that the network and Internet were going to be important and looked for software in that area. At the time, Lotus was already a successful company and IBM acquired it through a hostile takeover for the first time in its history. It turned out to be a multibillion-dollar business for IBM and enjoyed great synergies with the professional services business.

This set a precedence for buying software companies that the services branch could integrate. IBM did not just buy any type of software; they steered clear of enterprise applications such as what SAP and Oracle were selling, perhaps because they had a huge business integrating these for customers. Instead they focused on so-called middleware, the software that was used to develop applications and tie together applications from different vendors. This type of software corresponds to Platform as a Service (PaaS) in the cloud.

Another thing that proved very profitable for IBM was their hosting business. Many of their customers preferred not to have to deal with the systems themselves. Rather than trying to find highly specialized software specialists for a particular task, it was easier to have IBM run the whole thing. This is how outsourcing grew to be a big business for IBM.

Entering the Cloud

The IBM cloud grew out of its hosting business. It started in 2013, when IBM acquired the IaaS specialist SoftLayer. Their offering was more flexible than the competitors AWS, Azure, and Google, and it was more similar to hosting since the customer had more freedom to tailor the offering. In 2014 IBM unveiled its PaaS offering: Bluemix. It was built on the SoftLayer technology. These two brands made little progress in competing with AWS and Azure. In 2017, they were combined into the IBM cloud. The following year, IBM acquired Red Hat, which was the biggest enterprise open source company in the world. This was IBM's biggest acquisition ever and helped bring synergies to their cloud offering by helping boost hybrid cloud solutions.

IBM's Profile

Although IBM has a history far longer than most companies in the tech sector, it is still possible to see a common thread running through the company. In this section, we look at a few takeaways that reveal what kind of company IBM is and how they approach cloud computing.

Based on IBM's history, it is possible to extract a few insights into how they have acted and probably will continue to act. This is convenient to know in addition to their current offering so actual and potential customers can understand what to expect.

Recurring Revenue Rather Than Sales

Initially IBM preferred to rent out their equipment rather than sell it. Sales bonuses were calculated not on how much was sold, but on how much the salesperson increased the total annual recurring revenue of a customer. This continued with hosting, where IBM was and is one of the largest providers with more than 60 data centers around the world. Software support is similar. The switch to a service company based on consulting has changed that somewhat, but IBM is still a major player in software and hosting.

Preference for Big Customers

Throughout its history, IBM has sold expensive products with high margins, which means it focuses on the biggest consumers, as they are the only ones who could afford its products. This means that few if any companies have a bigger presence among the biggest companies of the world. They have cultivated their ability to communicate and engage with this type of customer. Conversely, it also means that IBM has little understanding of or appreciation for the needs of smaller companies. This can be seen in the launch of Bluemix aimed at this segment: it never took off.

Development, Patents Market Dominance

IBM has historically focused on developing intellectual property and protecting it. This instinct is designed to control and dominate a market that has served IBM well in the past, but has recently been challenged. IBM is still one of the top three companies holding the most hardware and software patents in the world though. This focus could be a contributing factor to how slowly it embraced the cloud, where open source software is much more prevalent. The recent acquisition of Red Hat, the world's largest open source company, signals a change in this respect.

Long-Term Relationship with Customers

IBM has, from its beginning, been obsessed with building relationships and understanding customers' needs. For example, one of the key metrics of managers at IBM in the 60s and 70s was monitoring the managers' time spent with customers regardless of whether they were in sales or engineering. Customers were also brought to IBM facilities for training. This has been a driving force in their development. It was the reason IBM moved from tabulating machines to the computer and it was why it developed the PC and set the industry standard for what that should look like.

Holistic Focus

IBM has historically been good at thinking about computing solutions holistically. Since their tabulating days, they have focused on customer training, field service, alliances with universities to build new and relevant computing skills and solutions, and on making sure that customer input was integrated with R&D, which in turn was integrated into manufacturing. This is why IBM set many of the computer standards we know of today.

Setting the Standards

IBM was involved in developing and defining standards in computing from the inception. Participation in industry organizations and standardization projects has always been encouraged. The SQL standard, ubiquitous in data management today, was due to the involvement of IBM. Historically, most standardization working groups have had at least one representative from IBM.

Dedication to Research

IBM has always invested heavily in research and today has one of the largest research divisions in the world, with 12 labs on 6 continents. Billions of dollars are spent every year on research in new technologies, such as artificial intelligence (AI), quantum computing, and blockchain. Five IBMers have received the Nobel Prize for work in semiconductors, scanning tunneling microscopes, and superconductivity. Even though IBM has been heavily involved in research and patents, they are not always good at getting things out in the market. This can also be said about AI, where they were the first to develop a program that could beat the Chess Grand Master Garry Kasparov and even win the game show *Jeopardy!,* but still failed to capture the AI market.

Fast Follower

While IBM was historically the driver behind important changes in computing, they were rarely at the bleeding edge in their go-to-market strategy. They preferred to wait to bring products to market until they had the patents. Their biggest successes like the mainframe and the PC shows this pattern: they were not first to invent the mainframe or the PC. They were better at tailoring them to their customers' needs and doing it in a comprehensive way, thereby setting de facto industry standards. Another example of something they didn't capitalize on is the relational database.

Ubiquitous Presence

IBM has viewed itself from the beginning as an agent in global politics. Through its history, IBM has cultivated relationships with all kinds of customers virtually everywhere in the world. It is not by coincidence that the name includes the word "international" and the old logo was a globe. The fact that IBM had relationships with major corporations around the world was a key factor in the IBM mainframe gaining dominance.

Summary

IBM is one of the brightest stars if history is taken into account. It has, time after time, established new industries and standards. With a heavy focus on the customers' needs, much of IBM's innovation has been driven by what the market wanted more than creating a vision for what the market needed. The close and attentive relationship has seen the company on a few occasions massively change their strategy in order to continue servicing their customers with what they needed. Compared to their competitors, however, they do not have the same agility and ethos of experimentation and market making. Some competitors, like Oracle and Microsoft, have been critically dependent on IBM for their fortunes. A treasure trove of patents and continued focus on basic research may keep IBM in the game for the foreseeable future.

This chapter explained how IBM developed from a hodgepodge assembly of companies that in one way or another produced machines for business customers. Focus on holistically understanding and servicing its customers propelled IBM along, thereby creating the modern computer and many of the standards used in the tech industry. Although it was late to the cloud industry, IBM's offering is a continuation of their focus on making it possible for customers to create computing solutions.

Oracle

Oracle Corporation has been a software giant for decades. From its beginnings as an American database vendor to a multinational enterprise software behemoth, it is one of the most polarizing companies in this market. In this chapter, we look at its history and how it shaped the company and its cloud offering. Oracle is one of the few companies that publicly espoused an anti-cloud attitude, but historically drove key technical developments that we today associate with the cloud.

The History of Oracle

Oracle was founded by Larry Ellison, Bob Miner, and Ed Oates in the summer of 1977. It was initially called Software Development Laboratories and the company worked primarily on consulting programming for other companies. Their first commercial product was a database. The three principals had been working on data management at a company called Ampex. Larry Ellison worked under Bob Miner and built a database called CODASYL on the PDP-11 minicomputer. In order to get out of the consulting business, they decided to build their own database. They looked through the technical literature and came across the British computer scientist Edgar Frank Codd's papers on the relational database from the early 70s. The relational database model allowed for a much more flexible and quicker way to store and retrieve data than the prevailing options at the time, which was the filesystem or the hierarchical database. Codd was employed by IBM and had been working on improving data management on the mainframe computer. IBM, however, did not initially implement his designs since their existing IMS database was bringing in a lot of revenue.

© Anders Lisdorf 2021
A. Lisdorf, *Cloud Computing Basics*,
https://doi.org/10.1007/978-1-4842-6921-3_5

Database Beginnings

Even though Ellison's co-founders were skeptical of this new approach, they agreed to build the system according to the relational model. They felt it was too risky to build it for the mainframe, since IBM heavily dominated that market. Instead they decided to build their system for the minicomputer, which enjoyed continuous popularity. The company name became Relational Software, Inc. The CIA hired them and funded the first version of the database. The PDP-11 minicomputer was heavily used in government circles, especially within the intelligence community. The minicomputer was more suitable for covert operations and could be brought on ships, submarines, or airplanes, something that was not possible with the enormous mainframes. Furthermore, the relational model, with its flexible access to data, was better for intelligence work. Within six months of the release of the first version of their database, called Oracle, RSI won several contracts with the NSA, the CIA, and Navy intelligence. The first version was built in Assembly and worked only on the PDP-11. The next version was built in the programming language that came to dominate low-level computing C. This made the database portable to any minicomputer running the UNIX operating system. Since this database became their primary product, they changed the company name to Oracle.

Oracle was not the only company pursuing a relational database. The University of California, Berkley had a research project called Ingres (Interactive Graphics Retrieval System). It was similarly the product of defense intelligence funding and competed with Oracle as the only two hardware-agnostic relational database companies. Up through the first half of the 80s, Ingres was considered a better product by many. However, in the latter half of the decade, they lost market share to Oracle due to a couple of factors. First of all the Oracle salesforce, which we will return to, was very effective in winning contracts. Second, they built their own language called QUEL. Since 1973, IBM had been promoting another language called Serial Query Language (SQL). When the American National Standard Institute (ANSI) was deciding on a standard for relational databases, SQL won, as it was heavily promoted by IBM. This meant that the Ingres database had to be rewritten to support SQL.

The Ingres research project was discontinued in the mid-1980s, but it spawned other companies in the database industry that came to haunt Oracle later. Sybase was founded by one of the developers of Ingres and its main competitor in later years. The first versions of Oracle's biggest commercial competitor today—MS SQL Server—were licensed from Sybase. The open source database PostgresSQL, which is the biggest enterprise-scale open source database rivaling Oracle for dominance, also traces back to the Ingres database. PostgresSQL is one of the biggest databases in the cloud today.

After defeating Ingres, Oracle spent the next couple of years competing with Sybase and Informix. Sybase offered a few features, such as read consistency and stored procedures, that Oracle did not. These were incorporated into the database over the following couple of years. This led to the programming language called PL/SQL, which allowed the database to take on more application-like functions and still permeates enterprises today. Over the years, Oracle regained technical leadership by focusing on clustering. This would eventually be marketed as the Oracle RAC. IBM built a relational database for the mainframe called DB2 that was very fast and efficient due to the higher technical specifications of the mainframe. However, with the clustering technology, Oracle around the turn of the millennium was able to show that placing inexpensive machines in a cluster gave even better performance.

Oracle's origins as a pure play software company were quite atypical at the time. The only major company pursuing the same strategy was Microsoft. This focus on software meant that there was no production or supply chain, which opened the door to one of the fiercest salesforces in the world.

The Fearsome Oracle Salesforce

Larry Ellison pursued a strategy copied by most Silicon Valley enterprises after him, that of hyperscaling growth in order to achieve market dominance. In order to do this, the focus was on building a salesforce that would sell no matter what it took. One of the good things about being a pure software company like Oracle is that once the software is developed, it does not cost very much to produce it. It just has distribution costs, which are negligible since it is a digital product. This means that the price is not set by the manufacturing costs, but by what the market will pay for it.

With a preference for high testosterone cowboy salespeople who would do anything, Oracle grew for many years by 100% per year. Ellison focused on developing the product and happily let sales be driven by someone else. Since sales fueled growth and product development, this was something that suited Ellison. But putting the legal department under sales was not a sustainable strategy. Oracle salespeople had a tendency to sell software at a heavily discounted price to reach sales targets and bonuses. In addition to this, ever more creative contracts were being drawn up. Since the legal department reported to sales, there was no one to check the contracts. Around 1991, this nearly led to the demise of the company. An alarming amount of customers weren't paying. A management shakeup and contract review led to massive write-downs of contracts. Some contracts did not even have a specified date by which payment was due and some customers did not even agree they had accepted to buy what the salesperson claimed.

This is why the Oracle salesforce was so feared, not least by Larry Ellison himself. Changes were made and the company survived and matured, but the culture of incomprehensible contracts, opaque sales involving future needs, and unhappy customers have persisted and followed them into the cloud. Today, they are the only one of the major cloud providers with a pricing structure that relies heavily on an opaque system of credits and discounts based on commitments toward future usage.

It almost happened again around the turn of the millennium, whereby sales had grown again to dominate the company's strategy under Ray Lane. Everything revolved around the need to make the next sale rather than building a bleeding-edge product. Larry Ellison took over again and steered the company clear toward a focus on the Internet and enterprise applications.

The Internet and the Future of Computing

It is a big mystery how Oracle missed out on being the undisputed leader of cloud computing. No one saw the importance of the Internet in general and enterprise applications in particular clearer than Larry Ellison. Before the dot-com bubble, Ellison was focused on the Internet as the future of computing. In truth, Oracle had no other reason than to do so, since they were one of the four companies driving the growth of the Internet, together with Sun Microsystems, which produced the servers, Cisco Systems, which produced the routers, and Intel Corporation, which produced the microprocessors. The Internet was still a consumer-based place, but every major company, from Amazon to eBay to Yahoo, was running Oracle databases to support their websites.

Perhaps as part of his spat with Microsoft, Ellison dreamed up a cheap network computer that would be a fifth of the price of a PC. This computer would just have a browser and all computing and data retrieval would be done on servers on the Internet. Such a computer was even built at the targeted price range, but unfortunately the price of the PC fell to the same range and it never took off. If this sounds familiar, it is because it is exactly what the Google Chromebook became 15 years later. Conceptually, there is no difference; it's a cheap computer with a minimal operating system that accesses the Internet through a browser.

That was the first example of how Oracle missed out on the cloud and was too far ahead of the market. The other was video on-demand. Oracle managed to produce a product around the same time that could bring video on-demand through the Internet. This was offered to customers as a test with a couple of network providers around the world. It was reasonably successful, but again it didn't take off until a decade later, when Netflix did exactly the same thing.

One Application to Run Your Business

Ellison had early on realized that the database business was limited in scope. He thought that Oracle, being great at managing data in general, should develop their capabilities in managing business data, in particular by building business applications. The undisputed leader in this field was the German company, SAP. Their S/3 product released at the start of the 90s was a suite of modules that supported major functional areas of a business. Oracle struggled to get into this market since the salesforce was used to talking only to technical people buying their database products. Applications were typically something bought by the C-suite, which Oracle did not have a lot of experience with. The application product did not materialize and was repeatedly postponed. This indirectly led to the second great crisis of the company, around 2000.

As a result of this, Ellison was forced to take over application development. This seemed to be quite a fluke. Ellison, who had already committed to the Internet, bet the whole application strategy on the Internet and making it available to customers through a web browser. Exactly who was first with that idea can be a matter of contention since PeopleSoft's version 8 released in 2000, as did another competitor, Siebel systems. They were similarly focused on being accessible through the Internet. Both were fierce competitors in the ERP and CRM market of enterprise applications. Both were founded and/or run by ex-Oracle employees and both ended up being taken over by Oracle. Oracle's product in the enterprise application space was called Oracle E-Business Suite and version 11i was the first comprehensive version built for the Internet (version 10.7 NCA and 11.0 in 1998 did focus on the Internet, but were not as comprehensive in terms of features). As part of the move toward running businesses on the Internet, Ellison led Oracle through the same process in tandem with developing and moving to 11i internally at Oracle.

The company, like many others at the time, was very fragmented in terms of systems. As part of the process of reengineering Oracle and moving toward an Internet model, Oracle succeeded in saving $1 billion. This was used to advertise 11i. Unfortunately, this came back to haunt them because they had not moved entirely to 11i. The beta testing done in advance of the release had been done for customers using internally hosted Oracle applications. This had shown that customers were satisfied, but upgrading and installing it at customers' data centers proved much more difficult.

This incidental discovery led to the realization that customers liked Oracle for hosting their Internet-based E-Business suite, paving the way for a large hosting business. Running enterprise applications on the Internet now sounds awfully close to the SaaS model, but somehow Oracle never made the transition. Maybe margins were too good with the hosting business or Ellison lost interest. It seems clear that all the pieces were in place for Oracle to become an SaaS powerhouse. It was up to yet another Oracle alumni, Marc Benioff, who started Salesforce in 1999, to deliver on that promise of a full-blown cloud business. Salesforce is today the biggest supplier of SaaS and important in the PaaS market too.

Hardware and Appliances and ... the Cloud

After the acquisition of Sun Microsystems in 2010, which was one of the biggest suppliers of powerful servers on the Internet, Oracle seems to have veered in the direction championed by Apple. That is, controlling the entire stack from hardware to software to make sure that the product was optimal. An example of this was the Oracle Exadata platform, which was an appliance that sported the fastest and biggest data management capabilities on the planet. This quickly became the flagship product that the company revolved around.

In parallel, the application business developed the SaaS model. They have shown the same willingness to consolidate in that market as they had earlier, by acquiring top SaaS vendors that fit into the market, such as RightNow (CRM), Taleo (talent management), and NetSuite (ERP). When Oracle acquires a company, they have a tendency to try to integrate the technology into the Oracle stack so that it is seamless. Their deep history in application development and the Internet has given them a clear lead over the other big five cloud vendors in the SaaS space.

After publicly deriding the cloud as a meaningless fad for many years, exemplified by the quote, "The cloud is just someone else's computer" (even today you will see Oracle employees and partners sporting T-shirts with this slogan), Oracle gave in and created the Oracle Cloud Infrastructure. Ellison complained for years (partially correctly) that the cloud was what Oracle was already doing. It is only partially correct because it was a hosting model where on-demand and self service was not possible. It wasn't until the 2010s that Oracle began to offer an Infrastructure as a Service (IaaS) offering in the shape of the Oracle Cloud Infrastructure (OCI). In 2018, the generation 2 came out and will gradually supplant the original OCI. There is no doubt that Ellison personally saw the future in Software as a Service (SaaS), having invested in Salesforce and NetSuite, but Infrastructure as a Service (IaaS) and Platform as a Service (PaaS) was never on his agenda. This is also why they are playing catch-up in these areas.

Oracle Cloud

Oracle launched their cloud offering by the end of 2016. It was called "Oracle Bare Metal Cloud" and it offered basic infrastructure services such as virtual machines, networking, and containers. It was later rebranded into the current Oracle Cloud. A second cloud offering was built in parallel under the same name, which Oracle calls the Generation 2 Cloud. There is no relation between the two offerings and the first one is being phased out, while Generation 2 was expanded to include more products. The solutions offered and pricing structure have shifted significantly in the history of the Oracle Cloud, leaving customers stranded with earlier versions and no clear migration path, which indicates that the development of the cloud platform still needs to mature and find its final form. The wide range of Oracle SaaS products run on the same infrastructure, but their development has been in parallel with the Oracle Cloud Infrastructure and should be considered something separate.

Oracle's Profile

Perhaps due to their great success in hosting and focus on delivering so-called engineered systems, Oracle was long reluctant to join the cloud market. They felt that the cloud was just a marketing term and that they already offered everything that the cloud offered. They just called it something else. While this is only partially true, it meant that Oracle was late to the game and has been playing catch-up with the other major vendors.

The history of Oracle reveals a few key traits about their behavior that can be interesting to be aware of, since they may explain behavior and help generate expectations of future directions. They are also important to keep in mind when dealing with Oracle as a technology vendor.

Great Technological Vision

Oracle often has a good understanding of where the market is heading before customers and consultancies realize it. They saw that relational databases would be a key data management technology before anybody else dared to. They were the first to develop clustering technologies that could link multiple pieces of hardware together to form a unified computing infrastructure (something used extensively in the cloud today). And not least, they saw the importance of the Internet for the future of enterprise computing at a time when the Internet was only considered a consumer-oriented novelty.

A Focus on Cutting Edge Engineering

Oracle is the prototype Silicon Valley software company focusing on developing technologies that others had not even dreamed about yet. They have frequently invented the "new" before anyone else. From the beginning Oracle has been a champion of the Silicon Valley ethos of hiring smart people and getting out of their way, with a blind trust in brilliant engineers' ability to work out a solution to any problem. Expect Oracle to continue to be at the top in terms of technical ability in the areas they choose.

Exaggerated Marketing

Like other tech companies, Oracle has been known for frequently stretching the truth, even when it's at odds with reality. It has been a mainstay of Larry to single out a competitor to antagonize. The thinking behind this is that it keeps Oracle focused on delivering a market-leading product. However, the public claims about the competitors and about its own products have been known to be exaggerated, aggressive, and mendacious. In the early days, the target was other database and ERP companies, then it was Microsoft and IBM, and now it is AWS in their crosshairs. If you hear a claim by Oracle about AWS, you are advised to check the veracity before making any decision. Particularly the claim to deliver a cloud product, which is in many circumstances merely a slightly adapted hosting solution, should prompt potential customers to be attentive to all marketing claims and try them out for themselves.

Creative Sales

Although Oracle has come a long way from the heyday cowboy salesforce that almost took it down, they are still among the most creative when it comes to sales. They still sell plans that commit companies to buying something in the future at a present discount, whether they will need it or not. This is an old practice that goes back to their early days. Oracle is clearly trying to continue these opaque sales practices. In Oracle Cloud, it is not always clear what you are paying for.

Complex Contracts and Incentives

Their contracts can be very difficult to understand, although much has improved with increased use of standard contracts and validation by the legal department. Their aggressive license audits and willingness to take customers to court has created animosity. Amazon, for example, has moved to get rid of all Oracle technology and Google prohibits installation of Oracle software. Even though they are competitors, this is not the case for others like Microsoft, Google, and IBM. It is a good idea to consider expert help on Oracle contracts, even in the cloud.

A Willingness to Release Buggy Software Early

To be fair this is not something unique to traditional software companies, but they had great challenges historically with their database (version 6) and E-Business Suite (11i), which seriously threatened the company. Ellison himself has admitted they were released too early, but also stated that some issues will only be discovered by customers. That said, they have been known to grind through and keep working until the products work. In the cloud, this is critical because you are not in control of the software. Caution and testing should be applied to new products, which is also something Oracle themselves recommends.

Market Leader

Oracle has shown a desire to be the undisputed leader of markets they enter. This means that when Oracle enters a market, they mean it. Conversely, they have always been careful not to enter markets they felt they couldn't dominate. It may not work immediately but they will continue working at it until it does or buy the competition. This was the story with the initial applications division. It was not successful for many years (a decade). If the products are buggy, they will work through the bugs until they work according to their vision. If Oracle moves into a market, they do it after consideration and they expect to be the leader. So expect the products to improve until they are leading products or expect them to leave the market again.

Build or Buy and Integrate

Traditionally, Oracle focused on building features into their products rather than acquiring third-parties to fill the gap. This began to change around 2004, when Oracle acquired PeopleSoft and Siebel. However, rather than running these acquisitions as pure cash cows, it was in Oracle's DNA to integrate them into their suite of products in a comprehensive and thorough manner. Oracle prioritizes comprehensive and integrated products over best-of-breed patchwork on the product front. Whether they have always succeeded may be up for debate, but their intention is clear.

Summary

Oracle has been a visionary in the software business and often has an ability to spot where the market is going. They saw the potential of the cloud before any of the major cloud vendors, but decided that it was a marketing fad. In fact, they are now playing catch-up in the cloud market. Their previous focus on enterprise applications and supplying customers with one system to run their business meant they led the Software as a Service (SaaS) market for ERP systems. Combining technical brilliance with aggressive sales and marketing has driven Oracle for decades. From their humble database beginnings to one system to run your business, Oracle will probably find a strong position in the cloud if they manage the transition.

The challenge is to convert the significant on-premise install base to cloud revenue. This means solving technical issues as well as addressing business model challenges. Switching from one lucrative revenue model to another is a daunting challenge.

Microsoft

In order to understand Microsoft, it is important to understand the history of its founders, Paul Allen and Bill Gates. Gates especially has been a key driver of the company's development. Like other large companies, Microsoft has suffered through crises and overcame them. Along the way it has gone through stunning transformations too. From a focus on proprietary installed software for personal computers to a focus on enterprise cloud software and a newfound affection for open source, Microsoft has seemingly come a long way from its origins. However, the company also displays a great degree of continuity across the decades that it has operated.

The History of Microsoft

Paul Allen and Bill Gates were very young when they started tinkering with computers. While other hobbyists in the 1970s came to computers through a fascination with hardware, Allen and Gates never had any interest in that. At the time, there was no software industry. Software typically came preinstalled with the mainframe, which was still dominant at the time. If applications were needed, developers wrote custom applications. Allen and Gates were intent on creating just such an industry from the beginning.

© Anders Lisdorf 2021
A. Lisdorf, *Cloud Computing Basics*,
https://doi.org/10.1007/978-1-4842-6921-3_6

Software Will Rule the World

In the 70s, computers were not something people could get easy access to. They were very expensive; this was before the personal computer or even the minicomputer had taken off. Even for a comparatively wealthy private school like the one that Allen and Gates attended, a mainframe computer was outside the budget. Around this time, timesharing, whereby multiple users could get shared access to a mainframe computer and pay by the hour, was gaining in popularity. It was not cheap either, but afforded an alternative that their school could afford.

Paul Allen and Bill Gates' experience with computers thus came from working with a timesharing mainframe system from GE, called Mark II. It was a mainframe computer connected through a Teletype terminal through which orders could be entered and results received. The language they used was BASIC, which was a simple language developed by Dartmouth College (which had also developed the mainframe timesharing system). With two other friends, they founded the Lakeside Programmers Group, which worked on a variety of ventures in order to earn money for computer time.

The first gig they got was to test another mainframe timesharing system for the PDP-10. The deal was that they would try as hard as possible to crash the system, write down exactly what they did, and got paid with free time on the system, which was spent on creating games and other fun projects. This took Allen and Gates into the world of operating systems and they developed an understanding of how Assembly code, the code that works directly with the CPU, was used.

The next assignment was to create a payroll program. It had to be programmed in COBOL, a more complex language that Gates did not know. He was therefore frozen out. After weeks the rest of the group reached out to Gates for help because they could not make the needed progress. He accepted but only on the condition that he would be in charge of the whole operation, something that set the standard for the future. The issue was that the group did not have the ability to sufficiently understand the rules for deductibles and tax. This shows the combination of business and technology acumen that came to characterize Microsoft. Another early program they developed together was a class scheduling system for the Lakeside school, which they took over from a teacher. This is a similar hard problem of understanding and adapting a business problem to programming.

With the advent of the Intel 8008 microprocessor, computers became small enough to fit on a desktop. In 1974, the Altair 8800 was introduced. It was the first personal computer to achieve commercial success. Gates and Allen were able to develop a BASIC interpreter for the computer and got a licensing deal where they were paid for every computer sold with their software. This became their first product, but other similar software products soon followed. Microsoft's initial business was to make programming languages for the hardware. They did this for Fortran, BASIC, and COBOL.

Becoming the Operating System of the Personal Computer

The breakthrough for the company came when they engaged with IBM to deliver software for the personal computer. Initially, IBM wanted to license BASIC and other programming languages from Microsoft, but also asked Gates if he knew anyone who could supply them with an operating system. At the time, Microsoft did not make any operating system themselves, but rather worked with one called CP/M, which was developed by Bill Gates' childhood friend Gary Kildall. Gates put IBM in touch with him and they agreed to come to Monterey California to meet and discuss terms.

Various reasons have been given for the two parties failing to reach an agreement, including that Kildall was unwilling to sell his main product to IBM for a one-time payment rather than its usual royalty-based system. Whatever the truth, the IBM team returned to Bill Gates and asked if Microsoft could make an operating system for them instead. Paul Allen had a friend who had adapted Kildall's operating system to the newest Intel processor. He called this QDOS for Quick and Dirty Operating System. Allen initially agreed to license it but eventually bought it for $50,000. This would become the foundation for Microsoft's first operating system MS-DOS, which it licensed to IBM under the name PC-DOS. Gates and Allen were smart enough to see that the PC would be a commodity and their operating system would guarantee interoperability with other cheaper computers than IBM's.

Microsoft's biggest client in the early days was Apple, which meant that Gates frequently worked with Steve Jobs. Jobs was designing the Macintosh and wanted Microsoft's help with the graphical user interface. Jobs and Gates had both seen demonstrations from Xerox Parc of a graphical point-and-click interface, which Jobs had developed into a comprehensive vision of how the GUI should be. Microsoft was hired to help develop it, but was not allowed to use the concept with their own operating system for a year. This resulted in what was to become Microsoft's defining product: Microsoft Windows. Because of delays with the Macintosh, it ended up being announced first, which infuriated Steve Jobs and put an otherwise productive collaboration on freeze. The initial version was presented in 1985. While it had little of the functionality and elegance of the Macintosh operating system, Microsoft delivered a good enough product that quickly became the standard for the Non-Apple PC market.

Applications for Non-Programmers

Microsoft already had products that allowed users to write programs in the major programming languages of the day, but since the goal of the PC was to reach every home, clearly something more was needed to make it useable to non-programmers, which were the majority of the PC market. Microsoft was also the first company to supply a so-called WYSIWYG (What You See Is What You Get) graphical interface for text editing, in what would become Microsoft Word. They developed this for Apple, and it gave them the sense that it was important to supply other applications that non-programmers could use. Excel, for example, was developed for the MacOS, but not as the first spreadsheet application. That credit goes to VisiCalc for the Apple II. Excel shows how Microsoft was able to latch on to a successful concept and continually improve it until it became the standard.

Over the years, the same attention to applications that could be used by non-programmers resulted in another hit application: PowerPoint. It was acquired from the company Forethought. Other applications that we have forgotten today were also introduced but were not as successful. These include FrontPage, Accounting, and Binder. These applications were bundled and sold by Microsoft. The Microsoft Office bundle is still the standard today, now in the shape of Office 365 as one of Microsoft's biggest cloud products.

The Internet

Microsoft was late to the Internet. Bill Gates later admitted that it took them by surprise, but they quickly latched on by developing technologies to power the Internet revolution. Based on the success of the Windows operating system, Microsoft decided to branch into the server software market. Servers are technically similar to PCs in that they have a CPU and a similar architecture. But they have different requirements since they are built for different types of jobs, like powering a website or a transactional database. Microsoft developed the Windows NT operating system to support the requirements of servers that need to run 24/7 without interruption, such as webservers.

As was the case with applications, they were not the first with key technologies but followed quickly after and built on their ubiquity in the personal computer space. The Internet browser was a crucial piece of software, as it provided the interface to the World Wide Web. That was something the company that had provided the interface to the PC was bound to find interesting and in their wheelhouse. In order to quickly go to market, they approached the company Spyglass and licensed their browser. Microsoft marketed it under the name Internet Explorer. It was bundled with the Microsoft operating system and became the focus of a high-profile anti-trust case because it crushed the popular Netscape browser. Microsoft eventually lost that case.

Microsoft also developed other technologies for the Internet, such as their Internet Information Server (IIS). At the time, Microsoft was supporting more traffic to Microsoft.com than the freeware webserver they were using could handle. Consequently, they decided to build the IIS. It was included in the Windows NT operating system.

The server business kicked off Microsoft's second leg, the enterprise computing leg. More followed here, most notably the Microsoft SQL Server database that came to rival the dominant Oracle database and today is second only to it. As had happened often before, Microsoft identified a piece of software they wanted to sell to the market and figured out how best to do that. In this case, they entered into a license with Sybase, which at the time was a serious challenger to Oracle. Microsoft was now well on its way to building a ubiquitous presence in the enterprise world, just like it had done in the personal computing world, with products that were needed by virtually everyone, like the server and the database. Virtually no software on the Internet or in the enterprise can run without a server and a database. These are also the most frequently used product categories in the cloud.

Hitting Refresh

Growing into one of the biggest software companies on the planet, Microsoft also seemed to pursue every opportunity even vaguely related to software. They built a media presence with MSN and *Slate* magazine, entered the cell phone industry and bought Nokia, built the Xbox gaming console, and created the Encarta encyclopedia. Growth slowed in the 2010s, perhaps due to this excessive expansion into new areas that were hit and miss. Something had to be done.

In 2014, Steve Ballmer stepped down and a new CEO was appointed. The choice fell on an internal candidate: Satya Nadella. Before he came to Microsoft, he had worked at Sun Microsystems, one of the early giants of the Internet server business. At Microsoft, he became president of the server division and worked for other enterprise products. Seeing the success of the cloud, Steve Ballmer had appointed him head of search and advertising in 2008, before giving him the task of building an answer to the success of Amazon Web Services.

Appointing Nadella was an unambiguous indication that Microsoft would focus on enterprises and cloud as the future of the company. With Nadella also came new directions on core values. Microsoft had, from the beginning, a strained if not outright hostile relationship with open source. In the 70s, Gates had a confrontation with the Homebrew Computer Club, which made pirate copies of his BASIC interpreter. In the 90s, Microsoft contemplated taking Linux, an open source rival to their server operating systems, to court. But after the arrival of Nadella, these feelings changed. Microsoft supported Linux and became a contributor and joined the Linux foundation. Even open source alternatives to the Microsoft SQL Server database found their way into the growing cloud business.

Another example is Microsoft's attitude toward competitors. In earlier years, Microsoft attempted to crush them if possible, as the example of the Netscape browser shows. Under Nadella's direction, Microsoft switched to building partnerships with competitors instead of just competing against them.

Other existing values were boosted, such as the focus on being a development platform. They purchased GitHub, the world's largest code repository, and continually been expanded on Azure, with developer-oriented features.

Building the Cloud Platform for the Future

Microsoft's cloud platform called Azure was originally announced in 2008 with the code name "Project Red Dog." The Chief Architect after Bill Gates, Ray Ozzie, saw clearly that computing would move to the cloud and promised a cloud computing platform that would allow developers to move their applications to the cloud with the same interoperability that other Microsoft services provided.

It was not until 2010 that it was released for general availability. The selection of services was limited and it featured basic storage, computing and networking, SQL services, .NET services, as well as cloud versions of the popular Dynamics CRM and SharePoint. Initial reception was mixed, but continued focus has elevated Microsoft to the status of a major cloud computing provider.

Microsoft's Profile

Microsoft is a widely diversified company that competes in many seemingly unrelated markets, as you read previously. Still, it is possible to discern a number of threads that run through the history, which explain the company as it appears today.

From a beginning as a software company supplying products to be installed on other companies' hardware through diversifications in many directions, Microsoft has come full circle and is now offering software directly to customers through the cloud. Although the initial success was in the consumer market, delivering the tools and technologies that developers need to build solutions has always been at the heart of Microsoft. Their decades-long history allows us to examine a few traits that stand out.

Fast Follower

Microsoft has always been good at spotting important concepts and trends and predicting the direction of the market. The Windows based operating system is a good example. Apple was the first and executed it well, but only for their own computers. Microsoft followed quickly with a product that worked on all PCs that used the Intel microprocessor, which became the market standard. Similarly, Microsoft did not invent the relational database, but based on the success of Oracle, decided to enter the market with MS SQL Server, which came to dominate along with Oracle. The same can be said for the cloud: AWS was the first to demonstrate a robust market, and Microsoft realized that in 2008 and decided to follow. Today they are in the absolute top of the cloud industry.

Release Early and Repair

Microsoft has a history of releasing buggy software or something that does not have all the functionality expected in the marketplace, as exemplified by the Windows operating system. Following that, they work hard to improve and fix the shortcomings with consecutive releases and patches. This can take a while and often needs multiple product versions to get there. The philosophy is to develop the product in conjunction with customer demand in order to be in the market, rather than spend extra time to wait for the perfect version. The thinking seems to be that it is better to get it out there and then learn what else the market needs.

Ecosystem Builder

Microsoft is good at building full-service ecosystems. The .Net framework was built from the ground up as a rival to the then popular Java programming framework. Microsoft invented foundational technologies and programming languages that make it possible for developers to build any kind of application without ever exiting the Microsoft technology ecosystem. They have succeeded in integrating this into the cloud, with Azure services so developers can more or less seamlessly transition from an on-premise programming world to the cloud.

Enterprise Ready

Due to its focus on foundational software like the operating system, office suite, Microsoft SQL Server database, and the .Net programming framework, Microsoft has cultivated close relationships with enterprises of all sizes in all industries globally. This position is rivaled only by IBM. When it comes to enterprise applications, the focus is on small- and medium-sized businesses. An example is the ERP system market, where Microsoft's products never really competed with the big solutions from SAP and Oracle. However, Microsoft's varied portfolio has made certain that the salesforce has products for every type of enterprise customer.

Focus on Foundational Technologies

Beginning with supplying programming languages and operating systems, Microsoft has a good track record with foundational technologies that developers use to build solutions. When you think about the Office suite, it is actually also a foundational technology for virtually every office worker. Microsoft is good at spotting the building blocks like servers, databases, access control, etc. and supplying solutions that are adopted almost universally by developers to piece together solutions. This has extended into the cloud, where IaaS and PaaS supply all the foundational technologies to build new solutions.

Summary

Over the years, Microsoft seems to have engaged in everything related not only to their original focus of software but also the occasional experiment with hardware, as was the case with the Xbox. Microsoft has even cultivated media and advertising businesses. If Microsoft sees a market for something, they find a way to enter that market.

History shows three basic patterns for how they do that. They might try to copy the concept as best they can and gradually refine it. This is what they did with the Windows operating system and the Office suite. Or they might license it and improve or package it in a novel way, which is how they entered the operating system, database, and browser markets. They also develop offerings from the ground up, which was how the Xbox was created. Over the years, these different approaches have been used to varying degrees, but always with a keen view on having a product meet an identified opportunity.

Microsoft has never been afraid to experiment and bring new types of products to market. Many of them fall short of expectations. Microsoft typically reacts by trying to fix bugs and improve the product until it meets market needs. But they are also brave and savvy enough to discontinue a product if there is no market for it.

Microsoft has rarely been a visionary, bleeding-edge company that invented new features the customers never even knew they wanted. Rather, Microsoft has a keen sense of where the market is going even if sometimes, they are a bit late to the game, as the Internet and mobile experiences showed. Under the leadership of Nadella, the culture has shifted to one of partnerships and cooperation rather than antagonizing competitors and quashing open source initiatives.

Amazon

It is perhaps not readily apparent how an online retailer selling books and CDs came to give birth to the cloud computing industry. In previous chapters, you learned how several individuals and technology companies had hinted at cloud computing and built different pieces of it. Some even tried to market it, but it was not until Amazon put it all together and showed the vision for how to execute it that cloud computing materialized as a viable business. The history of Amazon is in many ways the history of the birth of cloud computing.

The History of Amazon

The story of Amazon is the story of its CEO and founder Jeff Bezos. He was a gifted child who could have excelled at pretty much anything. After finishing his master's degree in electrical engineering and computer science at Princeton University, Jeff Bezos' first job was with a FinTech startup. That ultimately didn't work out and he shifted to a corporate career that led him to the Wall Street company, D. E. Shaw & Co., founded by David E. Shaw. Although Bezos did not have any intention of working in finance, Shaw's background as a computer scientist and his character appealed to Bezos. Shaw was, as Bezos later described it, both right- and left-brained.

© Anders Lisdorf 2021
A. Lisdorf, *Cloud Computing Basics*,
https://doi.org/10.1007/978-1-4842-6921-3_7

Origins

D.E. Shaw & Co. was not the typical Wall Street hedge fund. It was one of a number of companies—like Renaissance and Bridgewater—that pioneered the use of data and computers to guide decisions and make money in financial markets. But D.E. Shaw & Co. was special in another sense, since it did not shy away from building and running companies itself. It did not even see itself as a hedge fund. It championed the use of science to determine the best decisions to make, something Bezos would take with him to Amazon. Another practice that set D.E. Shaw & Co. apart was its recruitment strategy. It went only after graduates from elite universities, which was common, but what wasn't common was that they went after generalists. Going through honor roll students at top universities, they would send out invitations for interviews, which would be conducted by a team at D.E. Shaw & Co. The focus on science and rigorous decision making, recruitment strategy, and other parts of the company culture made a lasting impression on Bezos and he would take a lot of it with him as seeds for Amazon.

In this environment, Bezos would thrive and develop as a leader. In four years, he worked his way up to become vice president. Around 1994, the opportunity of the Internet was presenting itself to the company. David Shaw had experience with the Internet and its predecessor ARPANET as a researcher, which contributed to his excitement about its possibilities. Bezos did not have the same first-hand experience, but was in charge of determining how the Internet could be used for business opportunities.

They brainstormed different ways business could thrive from the Internet. One idea was to make a free email service funded by commercials called Juno. This was built and later sold off. Another idea was a financial service that allowed users to trade stocks online called FarSight. Both examples show that the vision was there a decade before Gmail and online trading platforms such as Etoro and Robinhood became billion-dollar companies. It was however a third idea that would make the biggest difference. The idea was to build an Internet-based online store, called The Everything Store.

Bezos considered whether to stay in Wall Street and continue to make good money or take the leap and start a business himself. He opted for the latter and decided to try the idea of The Everything Store by himself. He told Shaw he was leaving but Shaw wanted him to build the company inside D.E. Shaw & Co. For Bezos, however, there was no turning back.

He left New York and went west to build The Everything Store. However, such a store could not start by offering everything to everybody, so he made a list of possible product categories to start with, including computer software, office supplies, apparel, and music. Eventually, he decided on books since they were a pure commodity. A book in one store was exactly the same as in another store. Another factor was that the distribution was simple, since there were only two major book distributors in the United States.

The company ended up being called Amazon because goods would flow through it like water through the greatest river on earth. Due to considerations around taxation, it was incorporated in Seattle rather than California, which was the common choice for Internet and software startups. Amazon was not the first company to sell things or even books online and they did not have a magic formula or a silver bullet that helped them succeed. Rather, the success was built on many small choices that would add up over time. One example was owing their own warehouses rather than outsourcing them. That allowed Amazon to have complete control of the packaging and shipping processes. Another was the relentless focus on customer experience, which saw them establish the most lenient return policy at the time. This was critical at a time when the Internet was not well known or trusted. All of these things put Amazon on track to become an online retail behemoth.

Surviving the Dot-Com Crash

Amazon spent the 90s building warehouses and its supply chain and optimizing execution. The framework was as a traditional retailer, where the only difference was that there was no physical storefront, just a virtual one. Energy went into building operations and distribution processes. But the dot-com crash in 2001 forced Amazon to rethink their business and adapt. Amazon was not yet profitable because it reinvested all it could into developing its business. It was therefore particularly vulnerable in a situation where capital was not as available as it had been during the dot-com heydays.

The first step designed to bring in capital was a deal with Toys "R" Us to sell their toys on Amazon. This not only brought volume and cash flow into the business, it also started Amazon on a trajectory to transform from a traditional retailer into a platform company. That is, a company that supplies a service or marketplace as an intermediary between buyers and sellers. The Amazon platform was a technology platform where buyers of an ever-expanding assortment of goods could find sellers.

Because Amazon came from the retail world, it was accustomed to low margins and high volume. When you sell a book, you earn very little. This is why it is important to sell many units. So, while established technology companies like Oracle only saw a slight drop in their profits, Amazon would be hit a lot harder in a down market. This meant that the only way for Amazon to increase their profitability would be to cut costs.

This had a couple of consequences that would turn out to have a large impact on the company. In 2002, Bezos came up with a response. He had always had the typical Silicon Valley philosophy—that it was better to have decentralized and autonomous teams than one large centralized corporate bureaucracy—but he took that one step further than most companies. First of all, Bezos eliminated one-on-ones with direct reports. This would cut out time usually spent on status updates and politics and make it available for tackling problems.

Next, he instituted the two-pizza-team rule. Every team at Amazon had to consist of a maximum of ten people, that is, the size two pizzas can feed. The teams should be autonomous and only be evaluated according to a fitness function. A fitness function is a term from evolutionary biology describing how fit an organism has to be to survive in its environment. This function had to be an actual measure that Bezos could follow and approve. An example is the team responsible for the search function on the Amazon website. For this team, the number of click-throughs after a search might be a fitness function. The more people clicked a product, the more fit they were at performing what they were intended to perform. To achieve this, they had complete autonomy. However, in practice it proved difficult for teams to always find that one equation that described what they were supposed to do. But the basic idea lingered.

Another famous optimization from the same period was the narrative. Bezos had grown tired of PowerPoint presentations because he felt it was easy to hide behind bullet points and not think ideas through. The consequence was that he forbade PowerPoint presentations and instituted the narrative. The person responsible for presenting an idea had to formulate it as a narrative and write it up as an essay. This would be distributed to the meeting attendants at the beginning of the meeting. 15 minutes or more would be spent reading the narrative. After an initial trial, a cap of six pages was placed on the narrative since some teams would hand in up to 60 pages. A further twist was that if the idea had to do with a product or feature, it would have to be written from the customer's point of view and describe how it would be perceived by the customer. The way to do this was to write it as a fictional press release for the finished product, which is still the standard format for all new ideas at Amazon.

Reorientation

Around 2003-2004, the success of technology companies like eBay and Google began to reflect badly on Amazon, since Wall Street began to see it as a just another retailer rather than a technology company. This meant their valuation dropped. Bezos was consequently intent on reorienting the company from a boring, barely profitable online retailer to an exciting technology company. This would have to be done through inventing their way out. Around this time, he established a development center in California in order to speed up innovation and more easily attract talent. Following the success of Google, search was a big focus, and the "search inside" feature was developed, along with many other technical ideas.

Amazon was now ten years old and its code was not smooth or coherent. The infrastructure was held together with "duct tape and WD-40 engineering," figuratively speaking. Every day was a fight to put out fires and make sure services were running. Amazon had taken over the management of the Target and Borders websites, which only exacerbated the challenges they had with infrastructure. The way out was to focus on simplification. It was during this period that Amazon rebuilt its technology infrastructure from big, clunky solutions to one based on independent and self-contained parts that could be easily connected. Upgrades or fixes of one part did not take down the whole solution, as long as it still acted in the same way toward other connected modules.

The process of simplifying the infrastructure was a success, but even though Amazon was probably among the best in the world when it came to procuring the needed infrastructure for internal teams, innovation was still being hindered. Often during the six-page narrative presentations to the senior team, Bezos heard that actual proof of concepts could not be done because the necessary infrastructure to try the new features or projects did not exist. After having tackled internal processes and establishing world class operations, it was time to focus on the technology.

Bezos was influenced by a book by Steve Grand called *Creation*. The book was based on Grand's experience building the game Creatures, which allowed players to build life on their computer based on basic building blocks and see how they evolved. The book described how to build intelligent artificial life by designing simple computational building blocks called primitives. These were seen as similar to genetic building blocks that created life. Life in turn would evolve by selection by the environment's selective forces. This was an idea already top of mind for Bezos since the autonomous teams were asked to provide a fitness function for the same reason. The purpose now was for Amazon to allow internal teams to quickly create services and let customers select which were fit and provide the selective pressure.

This meant Amazon had to supply the primitives that internal teams would need to quickly create these services for customers. Bezos carried out brainstorming sessions with engineers about what those primitives could be and ended up with a list. Each team would get one of these primitives to develop.

In parallel, Bezos had conversations with Tim O'Reilly about what had come to be known as Web 2.0, which was a more open web, engaging with customers more directly than the original one-directional web. With Web 2.0 came social layers and more integration across services. While it was not initially clear to Bezos what benefit it would provide to Amazon, he eventually became sold to the idea and provided Amazon listings as well as other pieces of information in an API, not only to internal developers but also to third-party developers. Amazon was opening up to the world and tools should be made available to developers. This coincided with the first Amazon developer conference. Amazon was on a path to be a true technology company.

Building Primitives

In late 2004, the company's IT infrastructure manager, Chris Pinkham, decided to return to his native South Africa. Instead of leaving the company, he was allowed to start a new development center in South Africa. He accepted and a brainstorming session identified several possible projects. The one they decided on was a service that allowed a developer to run any application on Amazon's servers. They planned to use the open source tool Xen. The effort would eventually become the Elastic Compute Cloud, or EC2, which would become the engine of cloud computing or more precisely, Infrastructure as a Service (IaaS). When you power on a PC or a server, it will provide you with power to compute. On this you can install and develop software. The EC2 service offered basic unlimited compute power like that offered by a regular personal computer or server.

Another team in the United States did not have the luxury of working half a world away, but was under the constant attention of Bezos. They worked on providing storage through web services. Infinite storage with no down time was the requirement. This became Simple Storage Service (S3), which allowed developers to store and retrieve any type of file through a web service. Storage had before that point been a property of the computer or network, so this was another huge leap forward.

Both services were released in 2006 and were immediately successful. Since compute and storage are some of the most basic primitives of any computer program, it hit right at the heart of quickly developing companies like startups. Rather than having to raise money from venture capitalists to buy enough machines, companies could just start creating applications and see if they worked and then scale them through self-service. This was transformative. Internal and external developers alike could run their programs on Amazon's computers for an hourly fee through a web service API. Bezos thought of this as a utility like electricity and wanted to offer it at discount rates in large volume, like Amazon did in its retail business. As such, Amazon helped startups create new cloud services. Established cloud companies like Netflix would move its infrastructure from their own data center. In this way Amazon would power the rise of cloud computing like no other company.

This was the start of Amazon Web Service (AWS) and was the first true cloud offering of IaaS. However, as with any new venture, it needed a leader. The search went on internally and the Harvard business graduate Andy Jassy was selected for the job. He would turn this into Amazon's most profitable business and finally prove what Bezos had been claiming all along, that Amazon was a technology company.

Amazon's Profile

Even though Amazon's history has been comparatively brief, it has experienced a number of changes along the way and has branched into many different business areas. There is some continuity from the earliest times that shines through its history. In this section, we single out a few common characteristics.

Business Over Technology

While technology companies have often been driven toward their businesses by a technical insight or invention, it seems like the opposite is true of Amazon. Whatever they have built technically it has been as a response to a business problem or opportunity. From the beginning, the Internet technology was used to address the business problem of selling things online. The six-page narrative made sure that there was always a clear business idea before anything was initiated. It is a technology company relying heavily on technological innovation, but the driver of decisions and investment is whether there is a business case, not whether the technology is exceptional or interesting.

Low Margins and High Volume

Technology companies, especially in the software industry, traditionally operate with high margins. When a software product is sold, it requires little if anything to produce and deliver once it is developed. When production costs are close to zero, only the development costs are relevant. That means it is possible to receive high margins. Since sales cycles are also long and typically tied to larger projects, the volume of units sold is comparatively low. The software industry has always been a low volume, high margin industry.

Amazon turned this around. They transplanted the retail philosophy of selling high volumes at low margins into the technology industry. This could only be achieved because there was no sales cycle for AWS. Customers purchase the cloud services by themselves online. Because of the economies of scale that large retailers also benefit from, Amazon can supply services at a discount compared to alternatives.

Decentralized and Autonomous Teams

The rule about two-pizza teams means that Amazon took a different route than most companies, which evolve a central hierarchy when they grow. Instead of building a greater organizational hierarchy with several layers of managers, smaller teams are entrusted with developing products and features autonomously. This aligns well with Amazon's focus on developing primitives that can be sufficiently managed by a single team. It also requires the teams to be more precise about the purpose of their work. The flip side of this is that there is no large degree of coordination toward a bigger plan: autonomous teams do not magically dream up a comprehensive vision.

Advance Through Experiments

Amazon has never been afraid to experiment and never been afraid to admit when an experiment failed. Bezos has a Darwinian approach to development where experiments are viewed as life forms. Only by getting them out there as quickly as possible in real life in front of customers can they learn if they are viable ideas. AWS in itself was based on experiments. First Amazon experimented with opening up its catalogue and other aspects to the Internet. Then they built primitives for infrastructure and finally put these experiments together as products to sell to customers.

Simple, Modular Design

Amazon Web Services started with the insight that it was necessary to develop primitives that could be combined and recombined to ever-evolving new creations. A product needs to make sense in and of itself and have well defined interfaces rather than being comprehensive and all encompassing. The simpler a product is, the more useful it is to create new and unexpected solutions. Good examples of this are the two initial services: EC2 and S3. EC2 provides compute power and S3 provides storage. Both are simple and well defined and have not evolved, as most other software solutions, into so-called *bloatware*, full of myriad features few of which customers actually need. They are still very basic modular products. The simplicity and modularity of products make them simpler to manage and more resilient. Other services developed by Amazon have been similarly simple and focused on one well defined function rather than continuously expanding the number of features.

Focus on the Customer Experience

If there is one thing that Amazon has been relentless about, it is their focus on the customer experience. There are plenty of examples whereby it's been prioritized over shareholder value and employee welfare. All companies need to be focused on customers to a certain degree; if they do not provide value, they will cease to exist. But Amazon integrated the customer experience into its core. Examples of this include the press release as the format for an idea. The press release describes how the finished product feels to the customer. Earlier examples are the liberal return policies and a continued drive toward making the prices lower by pressuring suppliers hard.

Technical Innovator and Open Source Contributor

Due to Amazon's focus on volume, they were faced with technical challenges that no other technology company had been faced with. While Microsoft did have some Internet traffic, neither they nor any other technology company had ever dealt with hundreds of thousands of online transactions per second. This meant that the technology Amazon needed for their use cases was simply not developed by any other technology company. Consequently, they had to start from scratch and develop certain technology components themselves. Many of these have subsequently been released either as design papers or as open source software projects. Amazon's pragmatic attitude toward technology as a mere means to an end coupled with its focus on low cost means that they are also a great user of open source projects. The first cloud product, EC2, was based on open source designs. Many current AWS products are simple cloud versions of common open source tools.

Summary

Amazon's origins as a retailer shows clearly in how it approached the cloud. Contrary to a traditional enterprise technology company, which will typically look for high margins and bigger sales of a limited number of products, Amazon sells at high volumes and low margins. Like a retailer, Amazon created a business around high volume, small margins, and a wide selection of products. They have never tried to make big comprehensive suites that supply all the needed functionality. Rather, their products were conceptualized as atomic. They have to make sense in and of themselves. What is also distinctive is that "making sense" is defined from the customer's perspective. From their inception, Amazon focused on the customer experience above all else.

This way of making products for primitives fits with the way they are sold, which also distinguishes Amazon from other enterprise technology companies like IBM, Oracle, and Microsoft, who have large salesforces and frequent interactions with customers to guide, educate, and sell solutions. This model works well with large customers who typically have greater bureaucracy and longer sales cycles.

Amazon in contrast decided to sell software services in small pieces that made sense by themselves and could be used with little or no instruction, because they were so simple. This fit perfectly with the small autonomous teams that they had internally at Amazon. These are prevalent in small and medium sized companies and even isolated teams in bigger companies. This is why the initial traction was with startups. This approach has changed significantly over the years, because Amazon has invested in training resources and even expanding the salesforce to attract bigger customers and government contracts.

Amazon's continued emphasis on quick expansion and experiments, coupled with a pragmatic sense of business has taken the company in many different directions and will probably continue to do so.

Google

Of all the major cloud vendors, perhaps Google is the one with the biggest brand recognition, due to its ubiquity and use by consumers. It is only surpassed by Apple as the most valuable brand according to Forbes. Google is also the youngest of the five cloud vendors. Few companies can be said to be more embedded in the Internet and its development. Whereas other companies adapted to the cloud, Google was born in the cloud and drove the development of many technologies that help power the cloud today. To understand how, let's consider how a small science project grew to be a dominating force in cloud computing.

The History of Google

Google was founded by the two Stanford graduates—Larry Page and Sergey Brin. Just as with many other tech company founders, they were brilliant in their fields.

The Science Project

Larry Page was the son of two computer scientists. His dad had even spent a sabbatical at Stanford where he had brought Larry with him to work when he was a child. Although his intelligence and imagination were clear from an early age, what stood out was Page's ambition in any matter. At Stanford he chose to work in the department's Human Computer Interface group. His main focus was on product development, where he would religiously adhere to usability guru Donald Norman's dictum: "The user is always right."

© Anders Lisdorf 2021
A. Lisdorf, *Cloud Computing Basics*,
https://doi.org/10.1007/978-1-4842-6921-3_8

Sergey Brin was born in Russia and immigrated to the United States at age 4. His father was a professor at the University of Maryland, where Sergey graduated from in just three years. At the age of 19, he started the Stanford PhD program as one of its youngest students ever. His interest was originally in math, but he switched to computer science. Even at Stanford he stood out to his professors.

When Page arrived at campus, the two became friends. They were both looking for thesis topics. Both had experience with PCs and were used to the Internet as a natural part of their lives. This put them in a special position compared to the other big cloud vendors, who had come to the Internet for one reason or another. Google was born there.

Brin and Page both had an academic frame of reference and were driven by a dream of organizing the world's information and making it accessible to everyone. Page wanted to understand the structure of information on the Internet and discovered that the links on web pages were similar in function to academic references. Based on this, he created a way to rank web pages by how many other pages pointed to it. This is similar to how scientific articles are valued: the more citations the more valuable and consequently trustworthy they are. This would help users understand whether a given web page was relevant. This was the origin of what came to be known as the PageRank. To build this for the Internet, it was necessary to have complete index of all web pages and their links. While this was by no means an impossible task at that time since the Internet was smaller, it was also not a trivial task. Luckily, Stanford was uniquely positioned and had the funds to support such an effort. Now Page and Brin had the data, but what could they do with it? They found it could be used for web search, to help rank the relevance of search results of a query.

Searching for a Thesis Subject

In order to understand the context, it is important to understand that Page and Brin did not invent web search. Far from it. But their twist on it is what defines Google even to this day. At this time (around the mid-90s), the most popular portal to the Internet was Yahoo!, which was a curated site divided into hierarchical categories. It was possible to search it, but this process was similar to looking something up in a Yellow Pages directory. In order to search, you had to guess the category. A much better alternative came at the end of 1995 from a search engine called AltaVista. One could be forgiven for thinking this was the product of another hot new startup, but it wasn't. It was built by a big, corporate company: Digital Equipment Corporation (DEC), the champion of the minicomputer. As the minicomputer had overtaken the mainframe, it was now being overtaken by the PC. DEC had the vision to establish a formidable R&D division called the Western Research Lab (which would supply Google with many key engineers in its early days). In this lab, a small group of forward-looking people built the AltaVista search engine. It was not originally seen internally as setting the world on fire. At the time of its launch it was by far the most comprehensive search engine on the Internet. Even today, people who remember the early times of the Internet have fond memories of AltaVista as the best way to find information on the Internet.

Other search engines came along and took up the competition. However, no one but Page and Brin used the information in the links in their search results, even though the idea was developed independently at an earlier point at least in two different instances. One of them was at IBM research, which was quick to connect the researcher with a patent lawyer and quick to ignore the technology as they did not see any value in it. The other was by a Chinese researcher at Dow Jones, who similarly did not see any value in it. But Page and Brin saw the value. With the help of Brin's mathematical abilities, they were able to build a search engine based on their index of the Internet. It put everything together in a way that completely blew away the competition at the time.

The original Google site with just a search box. It was at the time provocative in its simplicity and it served the function of loading quickly, which was more difficult at that time, due to low bandwidth connections. Indeed, speed was and would be a persistent obsession at Google. Page considered speed a key part of usability.

The Quest for Speed and Scale

While working on creating the index of the World Wide Web, Page and Brin tested the limits of the Stanford Internet connection. Since the amount of data kept rising, they were scavenged for computers around campus and were able to find unused PCs and reappropriate them for their project. In order to extend their budget, they also bought discounted computers that were broke but could be fixed. The constant inflow of new computers allowed them to scale. Finally, they realized that they did not have time to write up their PhD dissertations and finish their degree if they wanted to develop their idea. During the first cash-strapped years, they continued their preference for low-quality hardware because it allowed them to scale and offer their service at speed. These two concepts became centerpieces of the Google approach.

Making Money, Too Much of It

The Google search engine quickly became universally loved. There were other commercial search engines at the time, but none came close to Google in terms of relevant search results. Even though Page and Brin had never been concerned with making money, it was clear that they were going to need a plan for that if they were going to expand their organization of the world's information.

In order to get money from venture capital in order to buy more machines and hire more smart people, they needed a business plan. The initial business plan called for three revenue streams: Licensing the search technology, selling hardware for search, and selling advertising. Out of these, the advertising business was envisioned to be the clear minority.

Originally, they did not want to have any ads in their search, but they realized that with search you would be able to make targeted ads that the user might actually find useful. This was the beginning of search ads. They would initially sell only sponsored links at the top of search results, but soon realized that ads to the right of the search results did not seem too invasive. The product used to sell and create such ads was AdWords. It was a self-service product that anyone could use with just a credit card. It was not necessary to get in contact with an agent and pay an invoice. The company would create the ad and select search terms and the ad would be displayed for the terms where they were relevant. This was later expanded to any type of page with AdSense. This was immediately a success for the smallest businesses. Quickly, the advertising revenues started rolling in, to an extent that Google had to hide how much they were earning in order for competitors not to catch on and start invading their niche. That lasted until the IPO, when it was no longer possible to hide just how well Google was doing.

The young company had now almost completely turned to the minority revenue stream from the business plan. It was expanding quickly. As smart as Google was, several key features of their advertising business had been invented by a competitor called Overture. It was a publicly traded company that earned a lot of money through a deal with AOL with similar technology. Overture had just been too late to patent many of the key inventions like pay-per-click and auctions that customers liked. They were eventually bought by Yahoo!, which quickly lost ground to Google. In the mid-2000s, Google was basically in a position where the more people used the Internet, the more money they made.

Building Data Centers

From the beginning, Google faced significant infrastructure challenges. One episode in particular set them on a trajectory to build world class infrastructure operations. Around 2000, which was in the company's infancy, they discovered that the index of Internet web pages had not updated for months due to a technical error, which essentially meant that no new pages were being displayed in the search results. The problem was that the crawler kept breaking down because of hardware failure before it could finish. It was not even possible to run the index because the Internet had grown significantly, and the crawler could not cope with the volume.

This forced Google to rethink how information was processed and stored and resulted in the creation of the Google File System, a system that was distributed across big clusters of computers and was fault tolerant. This allowed Google to run its massive processing and data management on cheap commodity hardware that would often fail. At the time, the industry alternative was to use bigger and more powerful computers. Google's approach made their data centers more resilient and significantly cheaper.

While working on their research project, Page and Brin had built their own server rack using Legos. This would set the stage for Google's willingness to rethink everything around what a computer is. This was critical, since the hardware costs and the cost of running it were among the highest given the scale and expansion of the company.

Given the centrality of processing and data for Google, it was a key concern to lower not only computer costs, but also data center costs. Initially they rented space, which came with limitations on how you could set up your computers. None of the subcontractors were willing to work with Google on how to optimize the data center operations, so they started scouting for locations and began building a network of their own data centers around the world. That way, Google had full control of everything. It was also necessary to rent fiber going into these data centers, since Google was critically dependent on the Internet. This similarly set Google on a trajectory to buy strategic stretches of fiber and quickly became the biggest owner of optical fiber connections in the world.

Google consolidated and vertically integrated everything from the web page down to the fiber and data centers and was able to offer unmatched speed and scalability compared to its competitors.

Applications in the Cloud

Google had quickly achieved a position whereby more traffic on the Internet meant more traffic to its search engine, since it had become the de facto portal to the Internet for many consumers. The Internet *was* Google. The focus was still on consumers, since they were the ones who clicked the Internet ads that generated more or less all revenue for Google. Consequently, if Google could make the Internet experience faster and more valuable, it would be directly transferable to increased revenue.

The first thing they had their sights on was taking applications that consumers used on their desktops and moving them online. Prime among these was Microsoft's Office suite. Through a mixture of acquisitions and internal development, the core offering of the Office suite was developed and offered for free. Google Docs was a cloud version of Word, Google Sheets a cloud version of Excel, and Google Slides was a cloud version of PowerPoint. These and other applications were eventually bundled into G Suite (now called Google Workspace) and they appealed primarily to small- and medium-sized companies.

These are examples of how Google moved on-premise concepts seamlessly to the cloud. They were simple, fast, and free for consumers and were offered completely through self-service.

Building a browser was a logical step for a company so heavily promoting the Internet. It had been a wish since the beginning, but CEO Eric Schmidt thought it would be unwise at an early stage to pick a battle with Microsoft, who at that time had an interest in promoting their own Internet Explorer. Google consequently supported and developed on the open source Mozilla browser instead. When time was ripe, Google once again focused on speed and simplicity in how the browser should work. Thus the Chrome browser was born. With the advent of cheap laptops, Chrome was integrated into the chromebook.

Google had truly come full circle and vertically integrated everything from the computer in front of the consumer, to the portal to the Internet, fiber, and data centers. If anyone doubted Google was a formidable force in the cloud, it was now apparent.

However, with the exception of a few offerings of simple self-service utility applications, there was very little on offer for enterprises. Everything was tailored toward simplicity and self-service and appealed only to small- and mid-sized companies with very basic needs.

Entering the Cloud Platform Business

With the success of AWS and Google's already well-established prowess in running data centers and cloud services, it seemed logical to open another branch of business. Like AWS, Google was already providing standardized simple infrastructure services to its internal teams. In 2008, Google opened up for the AppEngine, which allowed third-party developers to build cloud-based applications written in Python using Google's infrastructure. It wasn't until 2011 that the service became generally available.

Google offered many of its internally developed software services as managed services rather than as infrastructure services. The focus was from the start on Platform as a Service, where services had to be easy for developers to use. Since Google, like Amazon, faced unique technical challenges that no other technology company had, they developed a number of fundamental technologies that have become standards in the tech industry. This is due to the fact that they have been a frequent contributor to open source development, whereby core technical innovations, or at least the principles of how they worked, were offered to the open source community. This results in a solid offering of services that align with languages and open source frameworks that are typically used in startups and technology companies.

Google's Profile

Few companies have seen as explosive growth as Google has. In a very short time, it has grown to be one of the biggest companies on the planet. Even with such a comparatively short history as Google's, it is possible to discern a few relatively distinct patterns in how it operates. Let's look at what the history teaches us.

Machines over Humans

From the beginning, Page and Brin had an uncompromising focus on allowing machines and algorithms to do all the work, without human intervention. If the algorithms produced anomalies in the search results, efforts would be made to correct the algorithms rather than have a team of humans monitor and amend "bad" search results. The same was true of the ad business. As soon as there was a viable product for self-service and algorithmically optimized ad placement, the product that relied on direct sales by human salespeople was discontinued. Regardless of the area of application, Google uses human intervention only when it is an absolute last resort. Even the design of their products such as AdWords is deliberately more machine-like look than human.

Its focus on the power of algorithms has placed Google in front when it comes to the development and use of artificial intelligence and machine learning technologies.

Usability over Features

Just as machines are preferred to humans in the operations of the business, the products put the user at center. While humans are not always right, the user is. Products need to be easy to use without any training or guidance. Usability is prioritized over feature richness. This can be seen by comparing Google Docs to Microsoft Word. Google Docs has only a few central features that are easy to use and understand, and Word has many more features and capabilities. The tradeoff is less functional richness. This is true of many products that Google has created: they are easy to use but allow users to do only the bare minimum of functions.

Speed and Scale

Since the beginning of the search engine, speed has been of the essence, and that can be seen directly in the design. In the early days of the Internet, bandwidths were many times smaller than they are today. This means that it would take a non-trivial amount of time to load a regular HTML page even with an average amount of text and very few images. The Google site had only a search box and would also return the time it took to fetch the results. The ventures into development of foundational software products like filesystems and databases were all aimed at improving the speed at which Google was operating.

The other half of the speed equation is the scale, since Google from the outset had an ambitious plan to organize the world's information. Everything is designed with scale in mind. The foray into making its own custom hardware involved making it easier and cheaper to scale to thousands of machines and keep up with the growing Internet. The same can be said of building data centers, which allow Google to benefit from economies of scale. All services and products are built for infinite scalability, where little else than adding more machines is needed. Vertical integration—where Google has products such as the Android operating system, Chromebook, and Chrome browser in front of the user over optical fiber connections, data centers, and custom hardware—ensures that no one else can deliver the speed and scale that Google can.

Technocracy

Given Google's preference for machines and algorithms and the trust it places in its engineers, its products can come across as odd to non-technical people. More than a few times this has landed Google in trouble with the public. As much technical prowess as it has, Google often has little understanding and tolerance for human factors. If a technical solution is found to be superior, there is little understanding as to why the public would not want it. Examples include Google Glass and their self-driving cars. Google feels and has historically been able to show the value of this technical approach, but society and the world are not always on board.

Open Source Driver

Few companies have driven open source development as much as Google has. While other cloud vendors, such as Amazon and Microsoft, are open to using open source and will sponsor it on occasions, Google is a positive contributor and has realized a plethora of projects that have changed their field. Many of the technologies, known as "Big Data," can be traced back to Google. It's a company of engineers and Google allows its employees to work on side projects. Some of these side projects eventually turn into projects that are released as open source. Google has released thousands of projects as open source over the years, many of which (like Kubernetes) have become standard technologies.

Long Tail

The initial success of Google as an advertising company was not in their ability to compete with larger advertising companies that worked with large companies. Rather, the defining success came with Google's self-service solution, AdWords. What was distinctive about Google's advertising business was that it opened its products to smaller companies. Subsequent solutions like the G Suite (now called Google Workspace) had a similar focus on self-service and smaller businesses. This has also been the default approach by the Google Cloud Platform, where little has been done to appeal to larger enterprises. This allowed Google to grow its business in the "long-tail," which had not typically been serviced.

In Beta Until Perfect

Google has released many products. Rather than just release products to customers once the engineers think they're done, they usually give the new product or feature to very few users, often internally. Only when they work well enough will they be opened to external users, typically by invitation, as was the case with Gmail. Only then will they be opened up, still with limitation to the wider public in beta. It is made clear that these are beta products, so users can expect changes and potential issues. Only after everything has been monitored and proven to be running at scale without issues for a long time will it lose its beta designation. This process will often take years. This contrasts with other cloud vendors, which have a history of releasing buggy software to see what happens and then gradually correcting it.

Summary

Originally motivated by a desire to organize data and make the world's information available to everyone, Google has made a significant contribution to the development of the Internet in general and to Internet technologies in particular. Although the focus has primarily been on the consumer segment, Google has gradually moved into the enterprise business. This was done through a focus on smaller companies that traditional advertising companies weren't interested in and supplying utility applications for businesses. This set the stage for their venture into the cloud as well. Lately, it seems that Google has tried to secure larger customers and focus on servicing larger enterprises in their cloud platform.

Google, backed by its primary business in online advertising with high margins, has the luxury of an almost infinite budget for experiments of all sorts. This has been cultivated in the company and led to several technological innovations that brought an edge to Google's business. Many of these innovations have been released as open source projects and have transformed the tech industry. Some are even the basis of cloud products offered by some of the other cloud vendors.

Google's focus has always been on superior solutions that rethink commonly established assumptions, which has resulted in radically new solutions that sometimes were blatant misses and sometimes transformative. Regardless, they always seek to drive technology forward in a novel way.

Cloud Vendor Profiles

Now that we have looked at the five big cloud vendors in isolation, we can start to make comparisons that will help us better understand the differences between them. There are many superficial similarities and differences, but it would quickly go too far to try to capture all of these. Rather, the approach taken here is to identify a few core underlying features that show the core differences that determine how they behave. These are customer orientation, vision, end user target, product packaging, and cloud focus. We go through the five selected aspects and, for each, characterize how vendors compare.

Cloud Profiling

Through the histories in the previous chapters, a pattern emerges that tells us something about how the big cloud vendors work and behave. As a shorthand to visualizing this pattern, I propose cloud profiling. It is built on a loose analogy in the sense that profiling helps determine individual characteristics and behavior. I selected five aspects that I think describe the profile and differences between the cloud vendors—customer orientation, vision, product packaging, end user target, and cloud focus (see Figure 9-1).

© Anders Lisdorf 2021
A. Lisdorf, *Cloud Computing Basics*,
https://doi.org/10.1007/978-1-4842-6921-3_9

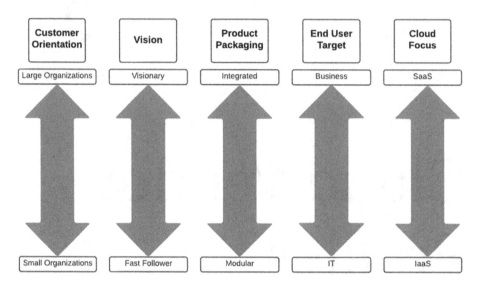

Figure 9-1. The cloud profile

Each of these aspects is conceptualized as a continuum where the two ends of the spectrum are described. It is difficult to measure these aspects in any stringent manner, so the chapter also indicates different points along the continuum and their relative positions.

Since all vendors have a variety of products and work with many different customer segments, it is not easy to say for each precisely where on the continuum they fall. For example, as far as customer orientation goes, nearly all vendors have customers along the entire continuum, but they will not have the same number of customers in terms of revenue. This is why each vendor is given a band across the five different aspects that denotes the focus or concentration of the company. This is done based on their complete portfolio of products and customers. Since this is not an easily quantifiable problem, special attention has been given to competitors, so that we see the differences. For example, IBM has always been focused on the biggest enterprises in the world and continues to be so, while Amazon grew popular with smaller startups and continues to be so. This does not mean that IBM does not have startup customers or that Amazon does not have Fortune 500 companies, they do. But in comparison, the number of customers and revenue generated across the company tells us that Amazon is more focused on startups and smaller companies and IBM on larger enterprises.

Customer Orientation

One of the most important aspects of a business is the customers they sell to. Customer segments differ significantly, and it is impossible to appeal to everybody. Some companies will claim that officially, but under closer scrutiny, it is clear that certain customer segments have higher priority in terms of marketing and incentives. The same is the case for the cloud vendors. They will all officially claim that they have the products for any type of customer, but once you look at their go-to-market strategies, product investments, sales, and marketing, another picture emerges.

There are also different ways to categorize businesses based on their customer base, such as considering if the company caters to the public or private sector. However, the most accurate telling category is to consider them based on customer size. A large company in the retail industry is more similar to a large financial services industry than a small retail startup, and the same is true for a large government agency. This has to do with organizational complexity being the same regardless of the purpose of the organization. Selling and marketing to large customers and small customers differ significantly in virtually all aspects, from sales processes to contracts to payment methods. If you approach a startup using a large enterprise sales process, it will fail and vice versa.

The customer orientation aspect is consequently aimed at assessing the size of the customers the company primarily targets. This will be a range from the largest multinationals to small startups. Although I recognize that a company may have customers who fall under all points of the customer orientation continuum, we focus on the customer segment that generates the most revenue.

Assessment

In Figure 9-2, at the bottom of the continuum with the smallest enterprises in focus, we have Amazon and Google. Amazon initiated the modern cloud computing platform and built the offering for their internal teams. These teams were more similar to startups or development teams in smaller companies. Consequently, the initial focus was on this group. It is a group that requires little if any direct sales and marketing. Everything was tailored to self-service, where a new customer could get started just by registering a credit card. This meant that the account structure was straight forward: one team, one administrator of everything, one credit card, and one account. The same can be said of Google, which was also focused on small- and medium-sized companies and relied exclusively on self-service.

This differs from how large or even medium-sized companies typically work. They don't typically do a Google search, create an account, and submit a credit card when they invest their million-dollar IT budgets. They have multiple divisions that need different products and different people responsible for managing different areas. That said, Amazon and Google are both trying to develop capabilities to address larger enterprises. Amazon has in particular ramped up their pre-sales and products to serve larger customers over the past few years. It is now possible to have complex account structures and, in certain parts of the world, Amazon helps larger customers with solution architecture expertise and a comprehensive training offering. Google does not appear to be as far along and still rely mainly on self-service. They also demo their products at conferences to assist customers, who mostly have to figure it out themselves.

Microsoft, IBM, and Oracle focus on mid- and large-sized customers. Microsoft, due to its wide range of exposure, tends to focus more on medium-sized companies, but that is also changing because of its cloud offering. Many large customers prefer the Microsoft cloud offering due to its structure. IBM and Oracle are working primarily to migrate their existing customer base of large- and medium-sized customers to the cloud from their on-premise offerings. Little marketing or sales is directed at startups, although you will see the occasional attempt. Microsoft is much better at this and small companies and startups are clearly also a focus of Microsoft.

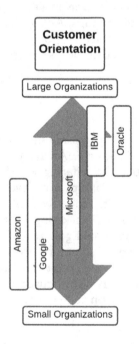

Figure 9-2. Customer orientation

Vision

The vision of a company in this regard expresses the degree to which a company is visionary, or bleeding-edge. Being visionary means seeing beyond the immediate needs of the market and being able to imagine future needs or wants. This is often independent of what the customers ask for and not something that focus groups or customer interviews drive. Apple's former CEO, Steve Jobs, did not spend a lot, if any, time interviewing customers about what they wanted. If he had, he probably would not have been driven to create the Apple products we know today. Instead, he had the vision to imagine a product and a future radically different from the present. This requires a special mindset, investment in R&D, and a tolerance for risk, since most visionary products fail.

Other companies follow after the visionaries, only when they can see a need for it in the marketplace. This does not by definition make them any less innovative. You can do something others are doing in a very innovative way. Furthermore, being visionary does not mean that you are necessarily going to be successful. Visionary products often fall short of consumer expectations. In fact, this is often the case. Tesla Motors did not produce the first electrical car. Not being visionary also does not mean that the company necessarily invests less in R&D, it is just a different kind of R&D, one that is aimed at maturing or improving a product.

The vision aspect can be conceptualized along the lines of Everett Roger's Diffusion of Innovation curve (see Figure 9-3), where a normal distribution describes the number of customers adopting an innovation. At the start of the curve is the group called the innovators and early adopters. These are the primary targets of visionary companies, although the rest follow along subsequently. Fast follower companies typically wait until they see that an innovation has started to penetrate the early adopter's category.

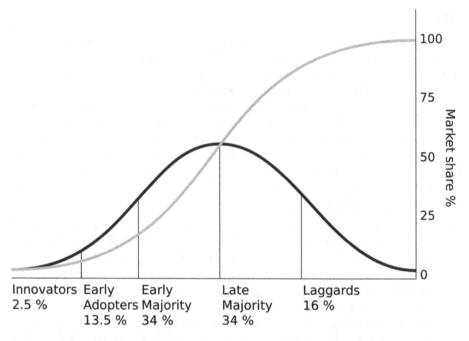

Figure 9-3. Diffusion of innovations[1]

The cloud is too new to have moved into the laggard stage, so no companies exist that focus on those groups. All cloud vendors are also innovative technology companies that garner their primary revenue selling new technologies to customers. The vision aspect therefore describes a continuum. At one end are the visionaries, with a focus on delivering cutting-edge products to the innovators and early adopters within the technology diffusion curve. The fast follower companies focus on delivering products to the early majority and late majority customers.

Assessment

In Figure 9-3, we see at the top of the scale Google. None of the other cloud vendors has developed as many visionary products, which is also seen by the failure rate. There are hundreds of Google projects and products that have been discontinued, all in the space of its two decades of existence. Google has also developed foundational technologies that have transformed computing in some areas like data processing. That does not mean that Google was always

---

[1]Image source: https://en.wikipedia.org/wiki/Diffusion_of_innovations#/media/ File:Diffusion_of_ideas.svg

the first to market. A couple of key technologies, like the use of links to index search results and pay-per-click auctions, were invented by others. They did not, however, set out to copy these but rather happened upon the ideas in parallel.

To a certain degree, the same can be said of Amazon. They also developed a number of visionary products, like the Kindle, EC2, and S3, but the investment in R&D seems more measured and willing to follow emerging market trends like the entrance into what streaming services and devices indicate. But since they created the cloud computing industry, few contest their vision.

Oracle is, even though it is an older company, also visionary and has continually tried to push the limits of technology. They have no issue with starting from scratch and trying to imagine what a product should be and then start building it. However, after the dot-com crash, their subsequent buying spree of companies turned the focus more to consolidating their market. Oracle also spent most of the 2010s claiming inaccurately that the cloud was just marketing hype for what it was already doing. This put Oracle on its heels in terms of the cloud, but it is in the company's history to be visionaries. It remains to be seen if they can emerge once again with visionary ideas.

Most people don't think about Microsoft as a bleeding-edge visionary. Even their most visionary product historically, the operating system, came from somewhere else. MS-DOS was purchased, and the Windows operating system was based on the Macintosh OS that Microsoft built for Apple. That does not mean they do not have visionary products like the Xbox and Kinect, but the products brought to market have fairly consistently followed successful products. They do this either by mimicking them or purchasing them. This ability to perfect products for the market need is incidentally what has made Microsoft one of the biggest technology companies in the world. That said, after Satya Nadella took over, real and significant attempts have been made to provide vision with the products that Microsoft offers.

IBM is in some ways similar to Microsoft, even though it seems to have been visionary in creating the modern computer industry—first with the mainframe and then with the PC. IBM always invests based on what their customers tell them, not what they thought their customers would need. Both the mainframe and PC existed before IBM entered the market. But there is an interesting twist to this, because few companies in the world have done as much basic research as IBM. This has resulted in a trove of patents and product ideas, but IBM has often failed to see the market potential for many of them. For example, they passed on similar search technology that Google later used to build their search engine. They simply couldn't find a way to bring it to market. Historically, IBM created the technologies that would set the stage for the computing industry, but others would often prove more successful in developing them into successful products. Another example of this is the relational database that IBM all but invented and Oracle developed into a visionary product. When it comes to the cloud, IBM seems happy to sit back and follow its competitors.

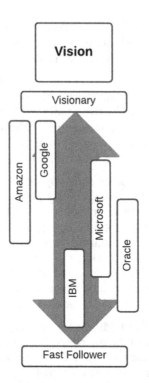

Figure 9-4. Vision

Product Packaging

The product packaging aspect tries to identify how products are packaged and sold. This aspect identifies what types of products are typically marketed by a company, not the literal packaging. Since we are talking about virtual software products, we have to think in metaphors.

Consider computers, for example. They can be built from scratch by buying all the components separately. One company packages each component individually and it is up to the customers to piece them together and install the necessary software. This is a very modular way of product packaging. Another company rents out fully furnished computers with software and subscriptions to streaming services. This is a very integrated approach to product packaging.

The product packaging continuum therefore goes from highly specific modular products to highly integrated suites. With a modular approach, the customer has to stitch the finished and fully functional product together by themselves, whereas the fully finished one will be delivered integrated and ready to be configured by the customer.

A module, however, is not a straightforward thing. The key here is whether the products sold are intended to function as small, independent modules or as big, integrated pieces of functionality. A module can be small or big too. In the example of computer assembly, individual chips can count as products, as can prebuilt motherboards.

This is why we need to think of product packaging as a continuum. Think of the size of a module as the number of features or functions it provides the customer. At the bottom we have simple ones like a messaging service that only allows sending of messages, and at the other we have an ERP system that allows a company to manage all of their core business functions. In between are products such as databases and BI tools.

Assessment

As can be seen from Figure 9-5, of all the major cloud vendors, none has more focus on the integrated suite approach than Oracle. This is the case for their ERP cloud and for their database. Rather than building new database products to market alongside the Oracle database, new functionality is integrated into the same database. The Oracle database consequently packs the same functionality that multiple different types of NoSQL databases do as well as the original relational database. This is done in an integrated fashion rather than by creating independent products and stitching them together.

IBM and Microsoft also have suites, but do not focus on that approach to the same extent as Oracle. They prefer to make modular products that can be used to develop new solutions. IBM switched to this approach in the 90s and Microsoft has a long history of delivering products that can be used standalone. Interestingly we can see that they are comfortable selling specialized databases like the Cosmo DB rather than integrating it in their flagship product, MS SQL Server, as Oracle did in their database.

At the other end of the scale, we have Google and Amazon. They focus on modular products. Even Google's attempt at an integrated suite, G Suite/ Google Workspace, is nothing more than a logical bundle of modular, individual products. Amazon has not attempted a suite, but contends to make the simplest, most resilient and robust products that could be used in multiple different settings. On this point, Google is on the same page with simple, user friendly modules.

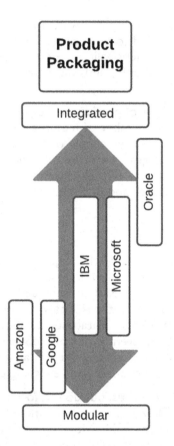

Figure 9-5. Product packaging

End User Target

Understanding what type of user a product is made for reveals a great deal about the design and purpose of that product, even if it seems to be the same product category. For example, a car is not just a car. If you are in the market for a car, it may make sense to look at the targeted end users. There is a vast difference between the user type of a Formula 1 racecar and a Ford F-150. If you need to haul timber or building materials over long distances every now and then, the Formula 1 is probably not the best option. The differences are perhaps not that stark when it comes to products in the cloud, but this example illustrates the dynamic.

Building products for developers who have years of experience interacting with computers through a terminal and building products for business analysts is similarly incompatible. A product for the developer is unintelligible to the business analyst, and a product for the business analyst is worthless to the developer.

When it comes to technology, it is common to talk about two primary groups of end users: business users and IT users. The IT group comprises all the technology people. They are the ones supplying the solutions that the business is using. The business group is the group working with those solutions to perform a business process. Both use technology. Both even create technology (the business analyst might create BI reports or Excel spreadsheets). The distinction between these two groups of end users used to be much clearer, but in the last decade the barriers have been broken down. New types of end users, such as data scientists, sit directly in between the two groups. This is why we view it as a continuum.

Each vendor can make a case that they have offerings for all the user groups, but they always focus on one of the areas in particular. This is why we indicate this focus as a continuum. The continuum goes from the tech-agnostic business user to the technically focused developer or system administrator.

Assessment

Looking at Figure 9-6, we can see that the company most focused on the business user is Oracle, with its portfolio of integrated suites of business applications. Oracle's goal is to make it possible to run the entire business with their products. But it is not just in their SaaS business applications we see this, even their data management products in the cloud have been targeted at business users and made it possible for them to perform fairly complex tasks that previously required coding skills.

IBM has a few products that are focused on business users for a number of specific use cases and industries, but its main focus has been on developer applications that support development. The bulk of its products are aimed at developers, which is a conscious decision they made as part of the company reorientation in the 90s, to move to a professional services company that builds solutions for customers.

Microsoft has an intermediary position with some products like PowerBI and Office 365, which entirely focus on business users. These are popular with many users and there is a real focus on marketing these to business users, but the bulk of Microsoft's products are aimed at developers. Their history has showed that they make products for developers. That starts with its early programming language products to operating systems and databases to the .NET Framework.

When it comes to Google and Amazon, it's fair to say that they are entirely focused on developers. Using their products requires you to understand a great deal of technology. Google has a few products that business users can and will use, but in the case of Amazon, this is rare.

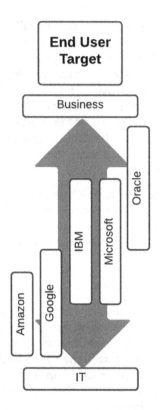

Figure 9-6. End user target

Cloud Focus

As you read in the introduction to this book, it is common to divide the cloud into three types: Infrastructure as a Service (IaaS), Platform as a Service (PaaS), and Software as a Service (SaaS). Similar to the other aspects mentioned here, it is not possible to focus successfully on all three areas.

It might not be as continuous a scale as with the other aspects, but it is in the sense that SaaS can be built on PaaS, which in turn can be built on IaaS. There are also emerging intermediary categories between these three, so it makes sense to talk about cloud focus as a scale.

At one end of the scale is SaaS, which offers a comprehensive solution that will support a complete business process. It often correlates with business users, as in the case of ERP systems, but it need not. GitHub, Function as a Service (FaaS), and virtually all products of the cloud company Atlassian are developer-focused.

In the middle, we have PaaS, with solutions like databases used by developers to build applications. At the other end of the scale, we have IaaS, which provides the most fundamental services.

The cloud vendors typically focus on one or two of these categories, but usually offer products in all of them.

Assessment

The vendor most clearly committed to Software as a Service (SaaS) is Oracle, as shown in Figure 9-7. None of the others comes close to the selection of products or market penetration. Oracle, due to its historical strength in middleware, is also building out its PaaS capabilities. It seems to have a focus on this, but does not currently have a comprehensive offering. The IaaS offering remains minimal and does not seem to be the focus.

For IBM, middleware has also traditionally been a focus area, whereby they compete with Oracle. It is similarly in the process of converting on-premise products to cloud PaaS products. Before the cloud took off, IBM dominated the hosting business and early investments in IaaS show that this is a key area for IBM.

Microsoft has a bigger interest in SaaS than IBM, but still remains focused on its development platforms. This means that its product development and sales efforts go into PaaS products like databases and IaaS in the form of virtual machines.

Google started out by focusing on PaaS and has continued down this route. It is possible to use Google infrastructure services, but its primary focus is on platform services like Big Table and Big Query. SaaS does weigh heavily too, but it's aimed at consumers. As Gmail shows, it's only as an afterthought converted to enterprises use.

Amazon has a rich variety of infrastructure services and platform services. These were both core services from the start, with EC2 (IaaS) and S3 (PaaS). There is virtually nothing in the Software as a Service (SaaS) area, but there could have been. If it were a focus of Amazon's, they could have built a pretty good SaaS online shop product.

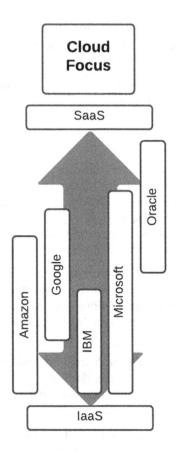

Figure 9-7. Cloud focus

Summary

This chapter discussed how the five areas—customer orientation, vision, product packaging, end user target, and cloud focus—can help us understand the five cloud vendors better. Each vendor has its own distinct profile, which can be seen in how it runs its business.

We can use this understanding to select the cloud vendors that best fit the needs of a particular company. For example, if a company is large and has few developers, Google and Amazon may not be the best place to look first. Conversely, if a new four-man startup needs to start developing, odds are that IBM is not a great match. The same methodology can be used for individual use cases. If the system will be used by business users rather than developers, certain vendors provide better solutions. This is something we return to in a later chapter, when we look at different cloud adoption patterns. Some vendors are better suited to certain patterns than others.

Cloud Technology

Although there are many aspects to the cloud, the most obvious one to consider is the technical aspect. This has naturally received a lot of attention and is often the focus of analysis and marketing. As a result, there is a plethora of information available about virtually every aspect of cloud technology. The purpose of this chapter is to provide an overview of the main technologies that we meet in the cloud. In the introduction, we saw that it is common to divide the cloud into three types: Infrastructure as a service (IaaS), which provides the most basic technologies; Platform as a Service (PaaS), which contains technologies for developers to create applications; and Software as a Service (SaaS), which offers finished applications to the end user. The emphasis here is on explaining basic structures and functions for the reader to explore in more detail elsewhere.

In order to get an overview of how these differ, let's look at the technological stack behind end user applications (see Figure 10-1).

© Anders Lisdorf 2021
A. Lisdorf, *Cloud Computing Basics*,
https://doi.org/10.1007/978-1-4842-6921-3_10

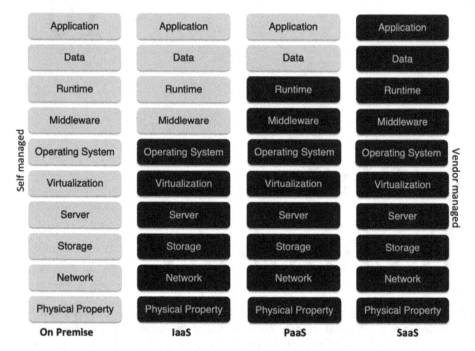

Figure 10-1. Management responsibility of technology stack in the cloud

The stack as described here is naturally simplified, but gives us a good idea about the differences between the different types of cloud computing. The left-most column in Figure 10-1 shows what companies have to manage if they run their own on-premise data centers. Going to the right shows the types of cloud computing, where the cloud vendor accepts increasing responsibility for the technological stack as you move right.

IaaS comes preinstalled with an operating system and the vendor manages its runtime. Customers can install anything they want, but have to maintain and upgrade that software. An example is a Linux virtual machine. PaaS offers a functional module that performs a particular function and typically stores and/ or manipulates data. The customer does not have access to the operating system and does not have to maintain and upgrade the application software, but can focus on writing the code necessary. An example is a database. For SaaS, the vendor manages everything related to running and maintaining the application. The customer is only responsible for configuring and using the software. An example of this is wordpress.com. Let's go into some more detail about these different types of services and learn more about how they are used.

Infrastructure Services

This section examines the fundamentals of cloud infrastructure. These are services that most directly mimic the components and structure of the on-premise data center. They can usually be mapped one-to-one and have a high degree of similarity across vendors. These are fundamental in another respect, since they are also the services that PaaS and SaaS run on.

The goal is for the reader to understand the basic concepts and components of cloud infrastructure. In order to do this, we will zoom in from geographical regions to data centers and at last focus on the core—that is, the computers that IaaS offers to customers.

Networks

Infrastructure is usually organized into regions of the world. Regions are more or less arbitrary geographical areas and can differ between vendors, but typically follow key markets like the EU, US, Asia, etc. In practice, the cloud vendors tend to partition their regions in a similar fashion. These regions contain availability zones. These zones roughly equal a data center, but may in fact consist of several physical data centers in close proximity. These are placed in the region, usually with a minimum distance of 60 kilometers between them in order to minimize the impact of a catastrophic event like a hurricane, flood, earthquake, or similar. If such an event occurs, there should be at least two other availability zones that can take over. Not all cloud providers have established this level of redundancy in all regions, but it is a common target. The infrastructure offered as part of the cloud vendors' IaaS are all defined by a virtual network within a region (see Figure 10-2).

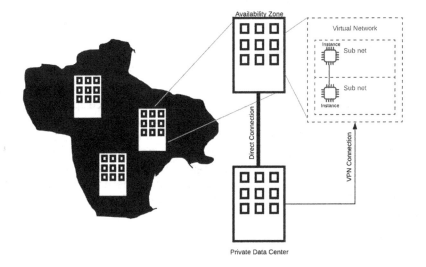

Figure 10-2. Geography of IaaS

The virtual network can be thought of as a logical grouping of infrastructure resources that connect to each other and exchange data. The resources are assigned an IP address and the virtual network defines the rules for which IP addresses can contact each other and how.

The customer can connect to the network in a few different ways. Either over the public Internet from individual computers or by a VPN gateway from the customer's data center. It can also be done through what is called *dark fiber*. This is a direct connection from the customer's data center through dedicated fiber to the cloud vendor's data center. The data thus does not travel through the Internet but through dedicated cables.

The virtual network can be further subdivided into subnets, which are further divided into units. This is typically done in order to allow a particular type of processing, either more closed off or more open to the Internet. As with the overall virtual network, particular traffic rules can be defined by these subnets.

The lowest level is the instance, which is some form of computer, either virtual or physical, that can be reached by a connection like SSH, RDP, VPN, or other. The connection allows instances to work together and the developers to install and manage software running on it.

Compute

The core of cloud computing is, perhaps not surprisingly, the concept of compute. The modern computer is defined by a couple of key functions. Understanding these will help greatly in understanding the selection of machines available from the cloud vendors. Different parts of their structure can be optimized for particular types of workloads.

The Anatomy of a Digital Computer

In order to understand the nature of compute, let's look at what a digital computer is (see Figure 10-3). First of all, it is important to notice the difference between storage and memory. It may at first glance appear identical, but storage is something external to the actual computer or server doing the processing. Consequently, data must be moved in and out of this storage. The hard disk on a PC is storage. There are two primary types of storage to be aware of. The traditional one is disk storage, where data is stored on magnetic disks that spin. The other is SSD, or solid-state disk, where there is no physical movement. SSD is faster, but also more expensive. Storage is measured in gigabytes.

A computer's memory is directly accessible and does not have to be written to and read from an external medium. It is consequently a lot faster than storage. On a PC, this equals the RAM. Memory is often measured in mebibytes (MiB). This is a binary measures of bytes, where one mebibyte is equal to 1048576 bytes or 1.048576 megabytes.

The concept of I/O covers the input and output operations from the computer. This is how the computer can communicate with peripherals like the keyboard, screen, printers, ports for communication, etc. It is measured by the amount of data going into and out of the server, typically in gigabits, and is also called network performance.

The control unit is a central coordinator interacting with the CPU. The CPU, or the Central Processing Unit, processes all the data. The other parts of the computer store and move the data, but only the CPU actually manipulates data. It is important to observe that most modern computers employ parallel processing, that is, processing is done by more than one CPU or core. Consequently, it is necessary to pay attention to the number of cores a machine has.

Another important parameter is the processing speed. This is the clocking frequency of the CPU and is measured in gigahertz, and it determines the speed with which it operates. This is measured in MIPS (million instructions per second) or FLOPS (floating point operations per second) for more scientific use cases. For CPUs, there are also two main types. The regular computer CPU and the GPU (Graphical Processing Unit). The GPU is significantly faster and more expensive.

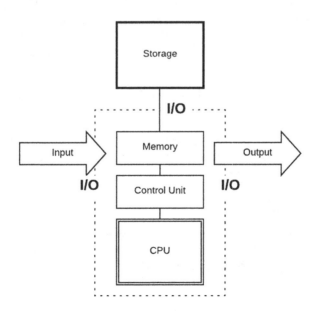

Figure 10-3. The anatomy of the modern computer

Types of Compute

Each of these parts of the computer can be optimized for different purposes. The cloud vendors offer different selections, but the following are the main types:

- General-purpose compute—This has average configurations for all the different parts. It is best for unpredictable workloads and consequently often used for test/development. Most types of applications and websites will also be good candidates for general-purpose compute, unless they have specific requirements such as high volumes of data or transactions or particularly taxing computations like graphics or complex algorithms.

- Compute optimized—This is where the number of cores or speed has been increased relative to the other parts. It could also be taking advantage of a GPU instead of a CPU. It is used when complex algorithmic operations are performed, such as processing unstructured data. That could be video transcoding, batch processing, or machine learning.

- Memory optimized—This is when the memory of the computer is optimized. It can hold more data in RAM and allows fast processing of many smaller units of data that swap in and out of memory. It's good for tasks with a high velocity of data, a lot of intermediate calculations, or real-time processing. Examples of this are fraud detection, IoT (Internet of Things), monitoring, and messaging.

- Storage optimized—This is when additional storage is attached directly to the machine. It is optimal for transactional tasks with a high volume of data without calculations where the results of the transactions need to be persisted. Such examples include point of sales, data warehouses, databases.

Types of Instances

There are different ways that the compute power can be made available to the costumer. Ranging from access to the complete physical machine to virtual slices with specific functionality preinstalled.

Bare-Metal Servers

A so-called bare-metal server is a single tenant physical machine, dedicated to the use of a single customer. It is close to a traditional hosting model and actually violates the requirement for pooled resources in the NIST definition of cloud computing, but since it is possible to procure it unilaterally in a self-service manner, many count it as a cloud service. Whatever we call it, it is offered by the major cloud vendors. It gives the customer direct access to the processor, memory, and storage on which an operating system can be installed. Virtual machines do not allow the same degree of control over basic machine configurations. It is consequently used for workloads that need deep access to hardware features or software that does not run on virtual servers. This could be either legacy servers or specialized custom workloads.

Virtual Machines

Virtual machines are the default type of compute offered by vendors. They run an operating system on top of hardware, but multiple virtual machines can run on it and they can be moved to other hardware. The customer has access to the OS, where executables (computer programs) can be installed and run. Since many customers are already running virtual machines in their own data center, it will be a familiar setup. The vendors also have a varying selection of virtual machines that come with preinstalled software on top of the operating system. These can be from third-party providers or a selection for a particular purpose offered by the vendor. It is also possible to make your own preconfigured custom machine image that you can reuse.

Virtual machines are used for standardized workloads where control of the entire software stack is needed. They are good for offloading on-premise data center workloads since many already use virtual machines. They are not used for certain types of legacy workloads, where control of deeper layers of the machine might be needed. The OS, including everything installed on the machine, needs to be maintained and patched with a certain frequency by the customer. Consequently, good PaaS alternatives to some specialized workloads exist. An example is databases, where it may be more work to maintain and manage the application on a virtual machine compared to having it done automatically by the vendor as a PaaS service.

Containers

A container is an abstraction on top of an OS that runs a preconfigured application with data. It is similar to a virtual machine but even more minimal since it shares the operating system with other containers running on the same machine. It can easily be moved to another container system either on-premise or in another cloud. It has many features similar to the machine image and comes with preconfigured applications and libraries. It often works as a complete application. A container is a standard way to package an application and its dependencies in an object. Containers share OSs with other containers running on the same machine, but run isolated processes. They are used when business logic and data can easily be isolated and run as a silo. They are ideal for microservices and ad hoc custom applications. They are not often used when the application logic has many non-standardized interfaces in a private network, like deep application integration with storage or filesystems.

Corresponding Compute Terms and Services

The five cloud vendors use slightly different terms for the same compute concepts. Use Table 10-1 to find the right term.

Table 10-1. Corresponding Cloud Infrastructure Terms

Concept	AWS	Azure	GCP	Oracle	IBM
Availability Zone	Availability Zone	Availability Zone	Zone	Availability Domain	Availability Zone
Virtual Network	Virtual Private Cloud (VPC)	Virtual Network (Vnet)	Google Virtual Private Cloud	Virtual Cloud Network	Virtual Private Cloud
Instance	Elastic Cloud Compute (EC2)	Virtual Machine	Virtual Machine Instance	Virtual Machine	Virtual Machine
Direct Connection	Direct Connect	Express Route	Google Cloud Interconnect	Fast Connect	Cloud Direct Link
VPN Connection	AWS Managed VPN	VPN Gateway	Cloud VPN	VPN Connect	IPsec VPN
	AWS VPN CloudHub	Data Gateway			
	Software VPN	Point to-Site			
		Site to-Site			

Storage

When it comes to storage, there are different types that are adapted for particular use cases with slightly different properties. They all support the same basic job of storing data, but do so using different interfaces and protocols.

- Block storage—Stores data in blocks. It acts much as a traditional hard drive on a PC. Any type of filesystem can be stored on block storage. It is used for extension of storage to compute instances that typically have little if any storage attached to them. Since it is close to the machine, i.e. the CPU, it has comparably low latency, but it degrades quickly in geographically distributed systems. Its flexibility and versatility make it good for virtual machines, boot volumes, supporting databases, and email servers, but it is also a more costly option than other storage alternatives.

- File storage—Stores data as files and folders in a hierarchical fashion in a filesystem. These files are accessed through a client program, where primary protocols are called NFS (UNIX and Linux) and SMB (Windows). The machines using the storage have to be in the same data center. The latency is higher than block storage but it's also cheaper. It is used for network attached storage systems (NAS), where typical use cases are enterprise file drives and big data storage.

- Object storage—Stores data as so-called objects, which are basically files of any size or form. There is sometimes no folder structure, just a list of files in a namespace. That means the structure has to be incorporated into the filename, which needs to be unique.

  Object storage is accessed through Internet protocols and thus far removed from the processor, which gives it high latency but good throughput. It is made in a way such that all data is replicated in a cluster of machines and is therefore redundant. If one physical machine breaks down, the data is still available on other machines. This provides an unparalleled resilience that other storage forms do not have by design.

  It is also the cheapest form of storage and is used by applications through a web service API, typically used for archiving, static websites, or data lakes.

Corresponding Storage Terms and Services

The five cloud vendors use slightly different terms for the same storage concepts. Use Table 10-2 to find the right term.

Table 10-2. Corresponding Storage Terms

Concept	AWS	Azure	GCP	Oracle	IBM
Block storage	Block storage	Blob block, page blob	Disk	Block volumes	Block storage
File storage	Elastic File System (EFS)	File share	File store	File storage	File storage
Object storage	Simple Storage Service (S3)	Blob storage	Cloud storage Blobstore	Object storage	Object storage

Platform Services

Platform services subsume a lot of the basic infrastructure components that we saw in the previous section. They provide a platform for developers to build and run applications, without the complexity of managing and maintaining the underlying infrastructure. PaaS supplies the full environment to develop, test, deploy, manage, and update custom applications. It allows developers to focus on writing code and increases the speed with which applications can be developed. The individual PaaS solutions may not always be possible to map one-to-one to on-premise installations and may differ across cloud vendors, but there are a few common categories of platform services that are easy to distinguish.

Data Services

Data is becoming one of the most valuable commodities in the modern world. One of the largest groups of platform services in cloud computing is data services, perhaps not surprisingly. Virtually any type of application needs to store and read data in some format. This means that there are many specific use cases that need to be supported. Let's look at the most common ones.

- RDBMS—The relational database management system used to be synonymous with the database and is still by a wide margin the most used system, due to its versatility and familiarity. The modern versions are based on the Structured Query Language (SQL), which many business users as well as developers are familiar with. There are many different products in this space, which Oracle and Microsoft used to dominate. They still hold a lead in the cloud, but this lead is diminishing due to capable open source alternatives like MySQL and PostgreSQL. Several vendors have versions of these even if they are sometimes branded differently.

- Data warehouse—A data warehouse is a database optimized for analytical use. Most frequently, it is an optimized relational database, but other examples such as column-based databases have also been used. The primary purpose is to make read access and queries of vast data volumes available for business intelligence. Since they are optimized for analytical use cases, they provide less flexibility but are still interfaced by applications and end users through SQL.

- Document DB—A document in this context should not be thought of in the typical sense but rather as a markup file format like JSON or XML. Document databases are optimized for storing, retrieving, and searching document type data structures. These are mostly used for in a web context, where JSON and XML are typical message formats exchanged through web services. It is not possible to access these through SQL and are therefore not often used directly by end users.

- Column DB—When data is simple in the sense that it does not vary a lot and it is not necessary to join data from multiple different tables, a columnar database might be preferable. It is optimized for single table data manipulation of very large volumes of data, such as transactions. In terms of functionality, it is scaled down compared to the relational database. Many things that are handled automatically by the relational database have to be programmed by the developer. But it makes up for it in speed and the ability to handle very large volumes of data.

- Graph DB—A graph in this context is the mathematical notion of a network of nodes. A graph database is optimized for network relationships and makes it easy and quick to query this particular type of data structure. Some problems are graphlike in nature, such as fraud detection and social network analysis for which the graph database is well suited.

- Key-Value store—There are many situations in application development where it is necessary to keep track of only two data points: a key and a value. The key is used to locate the data. A key-value store is a database optimized for simple pairing of a key and associated data. This can be used to retrieve a file like video or audio clips, or to keep track of internal application functions like the state of a session. It is often used in a web context.

Middleware

Middleware are software services designed to be used by applications. They are the glue that binds services together. For developers, middleware simplifies otherwise complex tasks that would have to be done again and again, like creating functions to exchange data between subsystems or manipulating data. These complex repetitive tasks are better subsumed in middleware, thereby allowing the developer to focus on the unique tasks the application has to do.

- Message queue—When building applications, it is often necessary to handle a continuous flow of messages between components and make sure they don't get lost and the system doesn't break down, even if there is a sudden surge in the volume of messages. This is what a message queue does. It decouples the transmission and reception of data from the processing of the data. The receiving module that does the processing doesn't have to be available and can get the message from the queue when it is ready.

- Streaming—This is a continuous feed of data points that sometimes can resemble a message queue, but it is simpler and does not have the same functionality as message queues. Streaming in a cloud context is not the same as media streaming. It is used in situations with high volumes of small, structured transactions, as is typically the case with IoT, messaging services, and server transactions.

- API management—An API is an application programming interface and in a web context it manages access to web services. Web services are the foundation of the Internet and how most modern web-based products implement their functions. It is therefore important to have one central place to manage access to all web services rather than doing that individually for each. API management also typically allows self-service and documentation of how to use the services.

- Integration and workflow—These are also typical needs when building an application. These services handle stepwise processing of data when a more complex workflow is needed. Integration is a ubiquitous need since data comes from and to external systems that have different formats. Data needs to be handled in order for the application to work properly with other systems.

- ETL processing—This is short for Extract, Transform, and Load. It takes data from source systems and prepares it for analytical access. It works with a data warehouse. It is a special case of integration that superficially resembles application integration, but there are differences since it usually runs in batches with high volumes of data and stores the data in a database.

Analytics

Along with increasing amounts of data comes an increasing need to make sense of that data. This is supported by a variety of analytics solutions offered by the cloud vendors. Some focus on processing and learning from the data while others focus on visualizing and discovering data.

- Big data processing—These are versions of software from the Hadoop ecosystem, which has been developed by the open source community. These solutions are designed to process and access very large amounts of data of any type. Since they are difficult to set up and manage, they have become popular PaaS offerings where the user does not have to do the same amount of management. Some services marketed as separate products are in reality open source solutions that are merely packaged and managed by the vendor.

- Machine learning framework—Allows the user to leverage machine learning without all the infrastructure. Even with the Hadoop ecosystem, there are many different components and it is possible to do data science. Some data scientists just want to write code and get the results or even to have the solution generate the code. With the increasing popularity of AI, machine learning frameworks are becoming popular.

- Visualization—Creates graphs and other types of visualization of data. Visualization is often the key in showing the patterns of the data. It is used for business intelligence reporting and can be embedded in websites for end users.

- Data discovery—Makes it possible to determine what data is available. If the potential users of the data are not aware of its existence or cannot find it, it is worthless. Consequently, products that supply data catalogs with descriptions and links to data source are gaining in popularity.

Application Services

There are a few functions that are repeatedly used in many different applications, which are convenient to handle in one system rather than program them for each individual application. Managing access by users is ubiquitous and other functions like search, email delivery, and notifications are also common. Some applications need more specific functions, like IoT and block chain. Many different solutions are offered as components to build applications faster and more reliably.

- Search—Allows users to search large amounts of data. This used to be a hard and specialized problem, but there are open source projects that have created solutions that are offered as packaged products by the cloud vendors. In some cases, these can even subsume the need for a database with all data being written to the search engine.

- Identity and Access Management (IAM)—Controls and manages user access to the platform and resources. With increased regulatory interest in protecting data, particularly personal data, it has become a key concern that any cloud solution have a centralized solution to manage users and what they can access. Integrating to a central IAM system offloads the responsibility to a system designed for this and the developer can focus on developing the functionality.

- Email delivery—Delivers email, which sounds simpler than it actually is. First of all, the system has to format the messages to the protocols used for email, which would be repetitive to do every time an email is sent. Second, it is important to make sure the email gets delivered. Today, a large portion of email is spam and it takes knowledge to make sure legitimate mail does not get caught by spam filters.

- Notification—Sends notifications to users' mobile devices or other systems. Many applications need to send notifications to users or systems quickly and reliably, which is what notification solutions do. Rather than program every time how to send notifications, the complexity is handled by the solution.

- Block chain—A technology that has seen plenty of optimism. It is also a complex solution to set up and maintain. Instead, PaaS allows users to build applications on a blockchain and integrate it into their application, without having to spend time learning all the details of how it works. For developers who want to explore the potential benefits, this is a good option compared to setting it up alone.

- IoT—More and more devices and their data feeds are being integrated into solutions and sensor data is often difficult to work with due to special formats and noisy data. IoT platform services make it easier to manage devices such as sensors. They also create a central solution that can serve as the backbone of IoT data integration, serving data in the right formats to applications.

Operational Services

In order to offer an application to end users, someone needs to deploy it. Once that is done, it enters a new lifecycle where the focus is on keeping it operational. This is done by monitoring the performance of the application. It also enters into a cycle of maintenance through upgrades and patches. All of these functions are also offered as PaaS.

- Deployment—Managing application code deployment is not as simple as clicking to install an app on your phone. There may be many steps that have to be carried out in a sequence. Keeping track of different versions is critical in order to be able to roll back if it turns out to have issues.

- DevOps tools—Allows continuous delivery of applications. This is used to increase the speed with which new functionality is delivered and orchestrates the different phases of the development, from writing the code to testing to deployment. That would usually involve many different tools, but DevOps integrates everything into one pipeline.

- Patch management—Ensures that infrastructure components are patched sufficiently in order to mitigate new and emerging security threats, but also to a lesser degree new or improved functionality in the component. It is time consuming to continually check if patches are needed and apply them. For certain security threats, it may be critical to do quickly.

- Monitoring—Monitors key infrastructure KPIs and proactively identifies issues with an application. For a number of use cases, it is critical that a solution run continuously, which is why monitoring performance is necessary. This can help in troubleshooting issues or proactively addressing them. Rather than building it for every single application, it makes sense to have a central framework like those offered in the cloud.

- Logging—Creates an audit trail of infrastructure and application events that can be used for everything from troubleshooting to performance optimization to customer insights. Applications can produce a lot of log information that can help reveal what is going on.

Serverless Functions

In some cases, it may make sense to completely skip building an application and just write the code to be triggered based on the rules of activation. This is becoming more common and lends itself well to small or at least atomic functions. Serverless means that the user does not have to worry about the runtime environment of the code, only the code that needs to be run.

Generic serverless code execution are isolated snippets of code that perform one function. It is often used when isolated pieces of logic need to be executed in connection with automated actions in an event-based architecture. An example is a trigger that indicates when new data appears and results in processing this data. They are also good for web services or for routing or formatting data, especially if this has to be done repeatedly. It is not good for more complex functions or functions that use a library.

Software Services

This section focuses on Software as a Service (SaaS) systems. This category is not usually treated along with the other types of cloud services and are approached differently by the different platform vendors. Some, like AWS, do not have many offerings, while others, like Oracle, have made it a major focus of their strategy. Since application needs can increasingly be solved by SaaS products rather than by building a custom application, it is important to understand what it is and how the market looks.

The market is quite different from IaaS and PaaS. There are many pure SaaS companies supplying vertically integrated business process support. The biggest pure SaaS companies, like Salesforce, Service Now, Zendesk, and Atlassian, all focus entirely on this and do not offer PaaS or IaaS. Many traditional enterprise application providers are also moving into the SaaS space, such as SAP, IFS or Infor, which is why it is a somewhat different category of cloud computing.

What Is Characteristic About SaaS?

Whereas IaaS is largely supplying a cloud version of your data center and PaaS is about speeding up development and delivery of custom applications, SaaS is about providing a fully functioning application that only needs customer configuration. This means that the flexibility is constrained compared to when you develop a custom application. Although some SaaS solutions allow provide opportunity for configuration, there are still limits to what it can reasonably do. An application for service management can be configured to support any type of business process that is similar, that is, one that involves handling requests and tasks in a workflow, but it would not be good for accounting, for example.

This means that SaaS differs from the other types of cloud computing in being constrained in its use to certain types of business processes. It is built to support a specific type of work, with specific types of terms used in the user interface. Sometimes, a selection of terms can be changed by the customer, but that is rare. A ticket in a service management system can't suddenly be changed to a container or a book in order to track containers or books. It does not mean that they cannot be used for it, but it does mean that such use would take a leap of imagination. In practice, however, an SaaS solution will be limited to a particular type of business process.

There are different approaches to how SaaS applications do that. The following sections discuss the most common.

Modular Solutions

Some SaaS solutions operate on a business function. Many such functions are used across different industries, such as recruitment, customer relationship management, customer support, online meetings, bookkeeping, payroll, etc. Even if industries differ widely in their business model and dynamics, they still need to support these functions. They need to hire people, keep track of and support customers, manage finances, and pay their employees. Such business functions show a high degree of similarity, which allows SaaS solutions to support them well, since the differences are within the bounds of what can be configured. SaaS solutions are therefore often offered as modular solutions to support well-defined business functions.

Human Resources

Without a staff, a company cannot function. Even though this staff is very different across industries, most key functions that need to be managed are similar. The following are typical areas handled by HR systems:

- Recruitment and talent management—Attracting the right people for the job and staffing positions internally requires tasks such as posting jobs, interviewing, and designing career paths.

- Benefits and compensation—The staff needs to be rewarded for their work, which is done through compensation and benefits. Creating the right incentives is important to attract and retain the best people.

- Payroll—As simple and trivial as it sounds, payroll is one of the most important functions. In some industries staff will walk out if they are not paid on time. The payroll function ensures that payment is made in accordance with benefits and compensation.

- HR information—The basic information about an employee, such as name, address, and social security number is recorded in the HR system. This is also where the organizational structure is maintained.

Finance and Accounting

Keeping track of funds and how they flow is a critical part of all companies, since banks and authorities hold them accountable for accuracy. Consequently, this is an important market for SaaS solutions. The following are among the most important functions.

- Accounting—Supports basic financial administrative processes like accounts payable, accounts receivable, general ledger, and purchasing.

- Planning and forecasting—Uses historical financial information to support the strategic direction of the company through planning future allocation of funds.

- Cash flow—Handles consolidations and budgets, tracks income and expenses, and monitors how funds are spent across different divisions.

- Reporting—Creates profit and loss statements, balance sheets, annual reports, and other relevant reporting to authorities.

Sales

The sales function is supported by Customer Relationship Management (CRM) systems. The most basic purpose of a CRM system is to keep track of existing and prospective customers and their engagement with the company. Sometimes customer engagements are small as single transactions, other times they are complex multimillion transactions between businesses. The first distinction is therefore between business to consumer (B2C) and business to business (B2B). CRM systems manage all the basic customer information as well as the sales pipeline and which products to offer customers. The primary features include the following:

- Lead management—Where prospective customers are being tracked and evaluated. This is where the sales cycle starts and ensures that they are developed in the optimal way and do not get lost.

- Contact management—Keeps track of the interactions the company has with the customer, enabling the sales representative to accurately remember the particular customer's situation and previous conversations.

- Pipeline management and forecasting—Once the first contact is made, careful attention is paid to how it is developed from a lead into a customer. This is done through pipeline management, which also allows forecasting of revenue.

Customer Service Support

The focus of support is to help existing customers resolve problems with a company's products or services. This is done with a customer support system. Like CRM, the support function also spans simple B2C and more complex B2B. Key features of such systems are the following:

- Omnichannel support—Customers are likely to engage with a company on many different channels, such as phone, email, and Facebook, and they expect the company to know about their previous conversations regardless of the channel.

- Self-service portal—In order to reduce the need for a customer service agent to engage with a customer and to optimized the speed of resolution, a self-service portal allows customers to find information to resolve the situation.

- Ticket system—To register the details of every support case and handle it to resolution, a ticket system creates a ticket that can be assigned to different support specialists and ensures the case will not be forgotten.

Marketing

The purpose of marketing is to promote the right products and services in the right places to the right customers at the right price. This includes traditional marketing methods as well as online efforts. It is important to have one system to administrate your marketing program and create an overview. The following are the most commonly used features of marketing solutions:

- Segmentation—Not all customers are alike. Consequently, it is necessary to segment them into groups that are similar relative to the product and marketing message. This is the purpose of segmentation. Many different pieces of information from demographic to behavioral can be part of a customer segment.

- Email marketing—Although multiple media efforts are used in marketing, email is still the most important way to reach potential customers. Creating campaigns, testing variants, and delivering mails are valuable features of email marketing.

- Social media management—Allows the company to create integrated campaigns across different social media platforms and track the efficiency. This is particularly useful because it allows more precise targeting based on identified customer segmentation.

Productivity

Allowing employees to write documents and presentations, plan and execute projects, work in teams, and communicate effectively are so ingrained in the modern work experience that we almost forget about them. These are some of the most ubiquitous SaaS products with the widest reach.

- Online meetings—Being able to meet online on different devices has become an integrated experience of the modern workplace. Scheduling and managing meetings of any size is handled by online meeting software.

- Document management—Creating and working on documents has for many years been done by sending documents back and forth, but document management solutions allow many different people to contribute and view documents.

- Project and task management—Whether it is a large project with many different participants or an individual employee's tasks, it is important to keep track of the work that needs to be done.

- Collaboration—Facilitating work together in geographically distributed teams is an increasingly important function in the modern enterprise. This is done by collecting communication and resources for the virtual team in the same place, and then allowing others to join the space.

Integrated Suites

Having many modules for different business functions from different vendors can quickly prove problematic, since they do not necessarily fit together. Integrating them in the cloud is challenging, just as it is on-premise. The standard solution developed for on-premise enterprise applications was to offer business functions as modules integrated in suites. Suites consist of several modules that are built to fit together in terms of the data and the interface. A company can start with one module, knowing that another exists in the suite that can easily be activated when the need arises. They are made to cover multifunctional areas that span different sections of a business.

The classic, most common type of suite is the ERP (enterprise resource planning) suite. This type covers all the functional areas needed to run a business. It is important for the different business units to be integrated. For example, to have the sales group sell products that the manufacturing group has or can make. The finance group needs to know how much value is tied in stock and how much is committed in purchase orders, as well how many sales are on the books but not paid yet. In order to make all these different functions connect, ERP systems provide modules integrated in a suite.

Even with suites in which the different business functions are integrated, there will be some work to configure and integrate and this may differ significantly across industries. Another approach is to support the integration vertically for a specific industry. Some SaaS vendors have created vertically integrated solutions for specific industries, like manufacturing and retail, where customers can handle all or most of their business within one system and without configuring or integrating any modules. Process and data are automatically integrated in the solution according to the particular needs of that industry, which makes it easy for the customer to adopt the solution.

Since these dynamics are not new in enterprise applications, there is a hybrid already developed for on-premise applications, where ideally the best of both worlds awaits. This is done by offering business functions as modules and vertical integration through suites with preconfigured templates for industry verticals. All these options come with tradeoffs in terms of flexibility and implementation complexity. The more flexible, the harder the implementation and vice versa.

Summary

This chapter explained how the cloud can be used to supply applications for end users. The most basic way is through IaaS, which is similar to moving a data center to the cloud. The vendor ensures that all the basic infrastructure is working and applications can be programmed much in the way they are on-premise. This provides the greatest level of flexibility for developers to optimize their applications. PaaS offers modular solutions for frequently occurring functions needed in applications and therefore relieves developers for having to maintain and develop the same functions again and again. This speeds up functionality delivery. It also means that it is less flexible in some respects. With SaaS, the application as a whole is already developed by the vendor. The customer can only configure it to particular needs. This means that it has the least degree of functionality and is only useful for a particular type of business process. On the other hand, it requires little effort to develop.

Securing the Cloud

This chapter highlights what it takes to secure the cloud. Some still consider the cloud an inherently dangerous and unsecure place, while others are moving to the cloud precisely because they think security is better there. It can be difficult to get your head around why both things can be true at the same time, but they can. It all has to do with how you approach cloud security. We look at it from a holistic, risk-based angle and go through the different classes of security services and features that cloud platforms usually offer. We also look at the security practices that must accompany cloud implementations. The goal is to understand how to secure the cloud properly.

What Does "Secure" Mean?

Having worked in the IT industry for a long time, I have more than once experienced these reassuring words after a sales pitch about a piece of software—"it is completely secure"—only to ponder what that entails. Although it sounds comforting, it is vacant and inconsequential. What does secure actually mean? Security requires in-depth analysis in order to arrive at a nuanced and adequate understanding of how to secure the cloud. Let's try to unpack the concept using the following four key observations.

© Anders Lisdorf 2021
A. Lisdorf, *Cloud Computing Basics*,
https://doi.org/10.1007/978-1-4842-6921-3_11

Security Is the Ability to Mitigate the Negative Impact of a System Breach

A breach can affect a system's confidentiality, integrity, or accessibility. An impact on a system is the negative effect of a security event. Just like other types of impact, it can be low or high. With a wide range of systems, there are different types of impacts. It is common to follow the National Institute of Technology's definition of impact in the document entitled, "Federal Information Processing Standard Publication 199" or FIPS 199.

FIPS 199 identifies four primary types of impact: business processes, organizational assets, financial loss, and harm to individuals.

Business processes are the processes an organization carries out to perform its purpose. This need not be commercial business, as in the case of NGOs, non-profits, or governmental organizations. Indeed, FIPS 199 is made for government. All organizations, public or private, have a mission whether stated or not. Some processes are more central to sustaining them than others. Organizational assets are material and immaterial things that an organization possesses. Financial loss is straightforward and can be conceptualized in the context of typical accounting practices. Harm to individuals is similarly straightforward.

A threat's impact level is reported as the highest result of the three different areas. If a threat has a high impact on business processes but is low on all others, it is reported as high. See Table 11-1 for details.

Table 11-1. FIPS 199 IMPACT Level

Impact Level	Business Processes	Organizational Assets	Financial Loss	Harm to Individuals
Low	Degradation in mission capability to an extent and duration that the organization can perform its primary functions, but the effectiveness of the functions is noticeably reduced	Minor damage	Minor	Minor
Moderate	Significant degradation in mission capability to an extent and duration that the organization is able to perform its primary functions, but the effectiveness of the functions is *significantly* reduced	Significant damage	Significant	Significant harm to individuals that does not involve loss of life or serious, life-threatening injuries

(continued)

Table 11-1. (*continued*)

Impact Level	Business Processes	Organizational Assets	Financial Loss	Harm to Individuals
High	A severe degradation in or loss of mission capability to an extent and duration that the organization cannot perform one or more of its primary functions	Major damage	Major	Catastrophic harm to individuals, involving loss of life or serious, life-threatening injuries

There are also different types of breaches. Again, following FIPS 199, it is common to distinguish the following key aspects of information security:

- Confidentiality—This is about keeping something a secret. "A loss of confidentiality is the unauthorized disclosure of information." An example of a loss of confidentiality was the leak of United States diplomatic cables. In 2010, WikiLeaks released communications sent to the U.S. State Department from U.S. consulates and embassies. What a country discusses internally is confidential and this leak consequently damaged U.S. credibility.

- Integrity—This is about the ability to keep information intact. "A loss of integrity is the unauthorized modification or destruction of information". Examples of integrity breaches include when government websites are hacked by special interest groups and propaganda is posted on the sites, rather than the official information. Another more subtle but impactful integrity breach is when a computer virus changes the receiving address in a bitcoin transaction. Since most people copy the address from somewhere else, the virus changes and inserts another address as the receiver.

- Accessibility—This is about keeping the system available. "A loss of availability is the disruption of access to or use of information or an information system." In 2017, logistics giant Mærsk fell prey to a ransomware attack. No information was disclosed or changed, that is, there was no loss of confidentiality or integrity. However, the ransomware attack encrypted more than 4,000 servers and more than 45,000 PCs, rendering them inaccessible to users. This led to losses in the area of $300 million.

Since security concerns the ability to mitigate such impacts, we need to consider how this is done. Mitigation efforts can be divided into tools and practices. Tools are the different technological solutions that can be used, such as those offered by the cloud vendors. These are rarely enough in themselves though.

Practices are the different ways we behave around, not only these security tools, but systems in general. We go into more detail about tools and practices next.

Mitigation Has a Cost

One point to keep in mind that might surprise some people is that all mitigation comes with a cost, even if it is manageable. Often, the cost is well worth the reduced risk, but until we realize the full cost, it's not clear that any given mitigation is helpful. Cost can be divided into three broad categories:

- Economic—Security always costs something and this is often the primary concern. Security tools cost money and security professionals don't work for free.

- Usability—Security controls like two-factor identification, CAPTCHA, and password restriction make the system harder to use. This annoys users and reflects poorly on the system. These are often a source of frustration when changing from an unsecure legacy system to a secure but cumbersome modern system.

- Time—Security procedures take time. Examples include sending a confirmation email, going through an approval flow, or configuring a system with proper protections, encryption, and checks. These all cause latency and adversely affect the system's responsiveness. All of these protections take time for users, system administrators, and developers alike.

You Can Never Achieve 100% Protection and Still Have a Useful System

I have worked many places where security discussions veered toward the inevitable conclusion that the only option that was completely safe was to turn off the server and unplug it. That seemed to be the only scenario that was deemed completely secure. In the cloud, the analogy is to prevent users from using the service for anything. This is, of course, absurd, but the point is that sensible people will always be able to point to one or another potential risk in any implementation. It is not difficult to think of something that can go wrong. If the objective is to be completely secure, the only way is not to allow the system to be used by anyone. This of course makes the system useless.

The Job at Hand Is Not Just to Secure But to Balance Security and Utility

The challenge is therefore not just to keep the system secure, but rather to find the right balance between security and utility. Since security is necessary in order to keep the system useful, mitigation will also diminish utility.

In order to find the balance, it is necessary to find the tradeoffs between utility and security. One type of mitigation will result in a lower probability of breach but will also reduce the utility, which is associated with economic cost, decreased usability, and extra time.

Sometimes even small reductions in usability can have huge impacts. For example, requiring two-factor authentication for online meetings would make them more secure, but it would make them more difficult to use. When people change phones, they would not be able to log in to meetings anymore. They would also have to spend extra time every time they joined a meeting. We need to contrast this with the added value of the mitigation.

With two-factor authentication, you reduce an already small probability of breaching confidentiality. The information is not typically sensitive, and a potential breach would not have a great impact. Impersonation is difficult if you are talking on camera. One might counter that not all online video calls use video, but then again if the discussion was important would you not require the participants to turn on their cameras? The tradeoff between the diminished utility and the increased value in this case seems to be negative. Now contrast this with an online banking system, where an employee can access accounts worth millions of Euro. Surely the added value of minimizing a breach is worth the diminished utility.

As these examples show, we can't say unequivocally that one particular security tool is the best, in and of itself. It is necessary to look holistically at the impact it will have on the system. Only with this type of analysis is it possible to suggest what security tools and practices would be best suited.

Security is not one property that a system has or does not have. It is also never the only aim, although it might superficially appear that way from public statements. Rather security is situational and depends on knowledge about the associated risks. It's about balancing security measures and their associated costs with the utility of the system.

This analysis can also help one understand the clashes that take place about information security in virtually all organizations in the world. IT security professionals are only rewarded for reduced risks, so they are not motivated to consider whether the costs to achieve that level of security are too high. Conversely, system users often only see security as something that negatively affects their ability to do their jobs, because they are rarely blamed when security is breached. The security professionals know little about the utility of a system, and businesspeople know little about the security aspects.

How Does Cloud Security Differ?

Our common sense tells us that security is about protecting our assets. Many will think in analogy to our homes, where we have walls, doors, and locks to protect our things. We close windows and doors. Maybe we even have alarms on them. This is perimeter security and keeping assets secure is tied to protecting the integrity of the perimeter. Once inside, little is protected because we assume the people allowed inside are okay. This is also how much on-premise security is conceptualized. The assets are physical servers, the firewall defines the perimeter, and a VPN or similar technology allows access from outside the physical premises. It is also frequently divided into different network segments with particular rules. They function like subdivisions of the perimeter.

In the cloud, this kind of thinking breaks down. We don't own the servers anymore and do not have physical access to them. They are now in the physical sense not in our perimeter. That does not mean that we cannot have similar functions for limiting traffic. This, however, only works for IaaS, because it resembles an on-premise data center that is run by someone else in the cloud.

Standard PaaS and SaaS do not fit this pattern. They cannot be walled in behind a firewall in the same way, but are fundamentally open to the Internet. This requires us to think about how to secure each service. The relaxed view of security that could work in an on-premise setting becomes a liability in the cloud. In principle, every component needs to be secured. Cloud security is more ubiquitous. Cloud vendors recommend that everything be closed by default and only opened for specific users and purposes.

The attack surface is many times higher in the cloud and attempted breaches presumably higher than most on-premise data centers. This also means that cloud vendors have a better chance at detecting new vulnerabilities than any individual company would. This makes the cloud safer because cloud vendors can patch and mitigate much faster than individual companies can. It also means that more tools are available to secure system resources.

Therefore, we can say that cloud security needs to be ubiquitous and built into every component. If that is done properly, it has the potential to be more secure than any on-premise installation. If, on the other hand, we keep the bad habits of on-premise deployments that worked only because they were sealed off from the surrounding world, we will have a much less secure system landscape on the cloud.

Tools for Securing the Cloud

Modern cloud vendors offer an increasing number of tools that allow customers to secure their cloud systems. We saw previously that security is not one-dimensional. Different tools address different aspects of security. In the following sections, we cover the major categories of tools commonly used to secure the cloud.

Identity and Access Management

Identity and access management (IAM) is a fundamental tool that even the smallest companies need. Its purpose is to have a central directory of identities or users in the organization and a record of what they are allowed to do in different systems, that is, their roles. This area is already standardized around a number of different protocols, which ensure that we have functions such as single sign-on and password reset.

A directory contains all its users and their credentials. This is the source that defines which users are valid. The cloud vendors all have at least one version of this. One of the most widespread systems is Microsoft's Active Directory (AD), so most vendors have a version of that or at least one that can integrate with a central AD. The directory can also contain other information about users, such as where they are working and their email and telephone.

In order to gain access to a system, an authentication needs to take place. This process verifies that users are who they say they are and that they are active. There are multiple ways to authenticate, the simplest via a username and password. More advanced ones include two-factor and biometric authentication. Access management systems handle user authentication.

When a user is authenticated, the system needs to know what that user is authorized to do inside a system. Identity management systems handle assignment and maintenance of roles for users in different systems. These systems maintain information about which roles and privileges are associated centrally with a user and synchronize that information with the systems the user is integrated with.

Traffic Management

A large part of the IT solution is made up of systems or components communicating with other systems or components. If the flow of information is not tightly controlled, it will be easy to breach the confidentiality and integrity of solutions. This is why traffic management is an important tool. The simplest example of traffic management is the use of access control lists (ACLs), which specify which IP addresses can access a given system resource or network segment. More sophisticated is the firewall. It specifies not only which IP addresses and ports are accessible by whom but also what type of traffic is acceptable. This is an important limitation that can control unwanted traffic if properly implemented. It can also prevent wanted traffic if not properly applied. The basic function of traffic management is to specify rules for how communication is allowed to take place within a virtual network and between it and the Internet.

Encryption

The purpose of encryption is to keep data confidential. Encryption is done with a cryptographic key. Encryption is particularly important in the cloud, where third parties store and transmit your data. There are different types of encryption with different strengths, but in the end, this is always the case.

It is common to talk about encryption in transit and at rest. The purpose of encrypting data in transit is to prevent wiretapping. Even if someone is listening in on the transmission, they will not be able to understand the nature of the communication if it is encrypted in transit. There are many tools and protocols for this type of encryption.

Encryption at rest aims at encrypting data stored on disk, whether in a database, on a filesystem, or on another type of storage medium. Here the threat is unauthorized access to the stored data. The encryption can be done manually, but many services encrypt the data by merely toggling a flag when configuring the database, for example.

But just as you don't want to lose the keys to your house, you don't want to lose the keys to your encryption. Unlike your house, it is not possible to call a locksmith to open your data if the encryption key is gone. That means the act of securing data against breaches of confidentiality may actually compromise accessibility if the key is lost. This is why key-management tools are popular. With key-management tools, you can store keys and rotate them with a certain frequency. This is important since it will change the key. If someone gains access to earlier keys, this will render them useless.

Security Assessment and Protection

One of the advantages of the cloud is that the vendors develop a good understanding of common threats. They know exactly what works in terms of security, much more so than any individual company would know. They also recognize emerging threats much faster. The advantages of economies of scale also apply in this context. Cloud vendors have turned this knowledge into products that are available to the customers. One type looks at the configuration of the infrastructure in the customers' account and identifies potential issues that the customer can subsequently rectify. It will look for things like open ports to the Internet and missing security patches as well as elevated privileges.

Other security assessment tools focus on data and can scan for sensitive data that may be out of place in databases or file shares without proper access control. There is a lot of regulation around data and these services can flag potential violations of these. This is also helpful from an auditing perspective.

The last way that vendors can turn their knowledge into products is through threat protection products. Perhaps the most well-known type is distributed denial of service (DDoS) protection. These tools can identify and mitigate DDoS. But there are also other types of attacks that are commonly carried out from the Internet that the tools can identify and mitigate.

Good Security Practices for the Cloud

As we saw previously, tools are not sufficient alone. Good security practices are just as important in order to secure the cloud. The following sections cover a few good security practices, although this list is not meant to be exhaustive. They are good to keep in mind in general, but particularly in the cloud.

Manage Your Data Securely

Managing data securely is closely tied to figuring out what data you have and classifying it. The first step is therefore creating an inventory of data in the cloud. Often, few people, if anyone knows what data there is. Data can be copied and forgotten, but if someone gains unauthorized access, it will be found. A data catalogue is a good way of creating insight into what data there is. This will help identify sensitive data. It means that an effort has to be made to classify the data. There are systems today that can automate parts of this process and identify types of data usually considered sensitive by regulatory regimes such as GDPR and HIPAA. That could include identifying where social security numbers are stored. But this is not sufficient, since it takes human knowledge to know where other types of sensitive information, like intellectual property, is stored. Therefore, classifying and cataloging data are important practices.

Minimize Access to System Resources

Managing access to the data is next. It is necessary to consider the granularity of access to data. Regulations are making it increasingly important to manage exactly what data an individual user can access.

System resources are servers, networks, and applications. Managing access to them is critical. At the most basic level, most system resources will have some sort of credential that allows users to access them. It can be a certificate, key, or username/password. These make the system secure if they are kept secret and only used in the intended way.

You must first consider what information users should have access to. Minimizing access to what is necessary is a good way to lower risk. Rather than allowing unrestricted access to a system resource, limit it to precisely what is necessary for this user. If a user needs to perform only one particular read operation, it should be limited to just that operation and not have complete administration privileges. However, it often proves difficult to determine exactly what privilege is needed to perform a particular action, which leads to assignment of elevated privileges to make it work. If you can do everything, you don't need to determine exactly what privilege you need. This can be done during the development process in the interest of speed and experimentation, but it's strongly discouraged in production settings.

For elevated privileges, the credentials should be managed tightly because they allow exactly the kind of system operations that malicious code needs to spread. This means that they should not be written into code or be stored on disks in clear text, but rather be protected somehow. Ideally, not even the developer writing the code has access to the credentials, but a central privileged access management service would.

Segregate Duties

Segregation of duties is mandated in certain industries, but is in general a good practice. In the context of system development, it means that people developing the systems must be different from the ones administering them in production. There are several reasons for this. First of all, this makes it possible to limit exposure to sensitive data. Second, changes to an application cannot be made unilaterally, which somewhat limits the ability to exploit a system. Third, it just makes more sense to have some people focus completely on having systems running according to their SLA in a robust and resilient manner and others developing new, innovative, and by definition, untested features.

Segregation is also used to separate duties of developers from those testing the finished systems. System testers are more efficient at uncovering flaws in the design and function of a system than the developer who created it. Due to confirmation bias, it is more difficult to look for evidence that something does not work properly than it is to find evidence that it works as intended. Vulnerabilities are thus more likely to appear in systems when there is no segregation of duties between the developers and testers.

Back Up Data

Backing up data is a way to make sure that system resources are available even in the face of catastrophic failure. This is a practice that has been necessary for decades and still often fails to be adequately addressed. The first challenge is to select exactly what to back up. Is it the whole solution, the data, or just enough so it can be reconstituted in the event of failure? The next issue is what the purpose of the backup is. Will it be used to recover the system from the latest backup point, or will it be needed to go back through different generations or versions of the system? Code versioning allows you to select an arbitrary version to recompile, but with data it might be more complicated. We also want to know how frequently the system needs to be backed up. How much data can we lose? One hour's worth, two days' worth, or more?

This is called the *Recovery Point Objective* (RPO). It may not be feasible to have multiple copies in the form of snapshots from one or more times a day, going back years even in the cloud. There are good reasons to maintain system snapshots as backups. Examples are ransomware attacks, whereby the breach is not realized until later. In this case, it is necessary to go back to an earlier version of the data without the virus. The last concern is the process of restoring the data. How long should this take?

This is called the *Recovery Time Objective* (RTO). For platform services, this is sometimes handled automatically, but it is necessary to make sure the default settings of RPO and RTO are sufficient for the use case or additional backup needs to be implemented. For many IaaS products, backup needs to be set up as much as it did on-premise.

Log and Review System Access

Logging involves much more than having a trace of what went wrong when a system crashes. While that is important, access logs can also be used to spot suspicious patterns and proactively counteract. It is similarly important for determining the extent of a breach in order to take efforts to communicate and mitigate them. Keeping a log is therefore the first step, but reviewing the logs is also important. It can be a daunting task, but there are solutions that automate this process. Many breaches today are so sophisticated that it can take months before they are discovered. Proper log review can help with early detection.

Logging is more than just machine-generated logs. Keeping logs of changes are just as important, since this can document decisions to deploy at a later stage. This points to the forensic use of logs when investigations are made after a breach or abuse has been discovered or suspected.

The last point about logs is to make sure that they cannot be altered. If they can be changed, their utility greatly diminishes. If a criminal can change the log, it has no real use.

Maintain Systems

The threat landscape changes continually, which requires solutions to keep evolving. This is especially the case in the cloud, where Internet connectivity makes everything more exposed. Bots and other automated systems are continually probing for vulnerabilities. Therefore, it is important to maintain systems so that they can cope with evolving potential threats. If this is not done, the system's confidentiality, integrity, and accessibility will eventually be compromised.

- Develop new functionality—An example of new functionality is two-factor authentication, which has gained in importance over the past few years. Applications that previously did not have that capability might need to add it. This is one type of system maintenance aimed at securing the solution.

- Upgrade and patch—A more traditional form of maintenance is upgrades and patches that are aimed at addressing identified vulnerabilities. The real challenge is making sure that solutions are continually updated and patched. Again, due to the nature of the cloud, a system that's not updated is more exposed than it might have been behind a company firewall.

Monitor and Prevent

Monitoring system performance is important to maintaining availability. If a server becomes overloaded or comes offline, it impacts the availability of the system. Monitoring can help detect situations when CPU or memory utilization increases beyond a threshold before it brings it down. The system can then can either notify operations or automatically bring additional system resources online. While the tools are there, they need to be configured.

Summary

This chapter explained that security is not a simple concept. It does not make sense to talk about any system being more or less secure without qualifying what that means. Security is about mitigating potential risks. That can be done with tools, which cloud vendors supply with ever-increasing sophistication. We have seen the primary groups of tools available. But tools are not sufficient to secure the cloud. Good security practices are also needed.

One key insight is that the cloud is neither secure nor insecure by itself. It doesn't make much sense to talk about any particular tool or practices as secure out of context. Even when security seems straightforward, we still have to balance the security measures with the cost of implementing them. This cost is not just monetary, but also includes the impacts of usability and time. Securing the cloud is about striking the right balance between security and utility/usability.

Cloud Economy

For all organizations, economy is an important driver, one that sets the limits for what is possible and provides future goals. The same is the case with cloud computing. For the cloud to be a viable option, it has to be economically attractive. In this chapter, we look at what that means and how the cloud can benefit an organization from an economic perspective. We also look at the practical consequences and consider the possibilities that exist for managing and optimizing the economy in the cloud. There are different features that allow organizations to get insight into and control the economy of cloud deployments. The goal of the chapter is to describe the major aspects and drivers of the cloud economy that make it worthwhile to adopt.

How the Cloud Can Impact an Organization's Economy

From an abstract point of view, a company's economy is evaluated in terms of profit. This is a fundamental measure that all companies are or will eventually be concerned with. If they don't make a profit eventually, it will be a problem. Profit is simply the revenue minus costs in a given period of time, such as a year or a quarter.

There can be multiple revenue streams and different business models. These differ greatly across businesses, which makes it difficult to say anything general about how the cloud can affect revenue. There are, however, three primary ways that the cloud can impact revenue. The first is through the agility of the company—its ability to adapt to changes in circumstances. The second is tied

© Anders Lisdorf 2021
A. Lisdorf, *Cloud Computing Basics*,
https://doi.org/10.1007/978-1-4842-6921-3_12

to customer retention, since retaining customers ensures continuing revenue, and the third is the ability to attract new customers.

The other half of the equation considers costs. There are two primary types: direct and indirect costs. We want to bring these down. The direct cost savings stem from spending less on comparable IT services. The indirect cost savings stem from increased efficiencies in the operation of the company. We discuss how using the cloud can increase revenue and reduce costs in this chapter.

But first a quick note on non-profit and governmental organizations. Given that their success as organizations is not directly tied to profit, it might seem that economic arguments are irrelevant. That is hardly the case. While non-profit and governmental organizations do not generate revenue in the same sense as a for-profit company does, their purpose is to maximize the effectiveness of the funds they receive. Since they still have costs, cost reduction is an important concern. The key difference between for-profit and non-profit (or not-for-profit) is therefore more emphasis on cost reduction.

Increasing Revenue

As mentioned, revenue is important to any company, but the cloud may impact it very differently across industries. If your company is working in the mining industry, odds are that the cloud is not going to have a profound effect on your revenue. If you are in online gaming, it may be a different situation. The following sections discuss three examples of how companies can boost their revenue by using the cloud.

Agility

Agility does not just mean agile development; it's a general ability to adjust quickly when circumstances change. These circumstances can be at the macro level, such as market shifts, or at the micro level, such as spikes in the utilization of system resources.

If we look at the micro level, agility is gained from a cloud system setup that quickly scales up when customer demand expands. This can be due to sales or sudden popularity. If the system resources do not scale with customer demand, customers will not be able to use the product and revenue will not increase as much as it might have. This kind of agility is important for companies that have large fluctuations in the utilization of their system resources.

At the macro level, the cloud helps the company deliver solutions that fit even subtle changes in market conditions. By leveraging the cloud, it is possible to develop solutions faster than with on-premise solutions. This type of agility is particularly useful for companies that are innovators and derive a significant part of their revenue from having more functional products.

Agility is important, but not always to the same extent. In industries where very little changes, agility is unlikely to increase revenue and may not be a primary motivator to move to cloud computing.

Customer Retention

Happy customers don't leave. That sounds fairly simple, but what makes customers happy? There are obviously many factors that go into making customers happy, most of which the cloud has little or no impact on. One area that the cloud does control is service availability. If the product is accessed through or dependent on the Internet, there is a good chance that the cloud can be significant in creating happy customers. One example that a lot of traditional on-premise software vendors are seeing is that customers want them to offer their service as a highly available solution, where they do not have to maintain and provision the servers necessary. Instead, the vendor handles it. Another aspect of availability is resilience. With the cloud it is possible to build highly resilient systems that quickly and easily fail over when they fail.

Another aspect of availability is latency or speed of the service. This similarly applies to services that depend on the Internet. The cloud allows companies access to more powerful computing resources more easily. A good example of this is with Internet sites. Providing a global presence with sub-second latency requires a company to have servers close to users all over the world. This is incredibly difficult to achieve singlehandedly by any individual organization. But the cloud providers offer this as a standard. In entertainment and e-commerce, customer retention may very well depend on the service's responsiveness. If the customer clicks and nothing happens fast enough, they may switch to a competitor.

When customer happiness is tied to the Internet, the cloud may be significant in retaining existing customers and thereby boosting revenue.

New Customers

When existing customers recommend a company to their peer group, that can result in new customers. There are many things that can lead to existing customers recommending a product or service. One is connectedness. The cloud is already connected to the Internet, which makes it trivial to integrate into social networks. Sharing results and integrating may be key to exposing the service to new potential customers. An example of this is HR recruitment. When job postings move online, the applicant is moved into the recruitment system, which creates awareness in the eyes of the applicant. Other examples of this approach are survey tools. It is common for cloud-based solutions to build in viral features that can help attract new customers.

Another way to attract new customers is by satisfaction. This is a lot more difficult to point to. In general, the convenience of cloud accessibility adds to the satisfaction of a product. If you can order online or with the click of a button, it is more convenient. It could also be an online assistant where the customer talks or chats with an AI helper to resolve issues. These are difficult for individual companies to train and provide, but many cloud providers provide them as standard features. More human interfaces may thus boost satisfaction.

Reducing Costs

Cost cutting is always a popular agenda with management and the cloud allows for plenty of such opportunities. The cloud is also different, both in terms of the dynamics of cost (operational expenditure compared to capital expenditure for on-premise) and in how it works. Cost cutting depends on the specifics of the case. There is no guarantee.

Direct Cost Savings

If you can get the same thing cheaper, you have a direct cost savings. It is not always so easy to make a direct comparison in the cloud. In the case of IaaS especially and some SaaS products, it does make sense to talk about a one-to-one replacement. For example, a virtual machine is the same when it runs in the cloud as when it runs on-premise. This makes it easy to calculate the cost savings. The same is the case for a database. However, when we talk about a finance system, it might not directly compare to an existing on-premise system and the direct savings might be difficult to calculate.

While direct cost savings are easier to calculate and build a business case on, there is one complication. The economics often move from capital expenses, where costs are realized up front at the time of purchase, to operational expenses, where they occur as the service is used. Whether one is cheaper than the other depends on how long the capital investment will depreciate, since this gives an average monthly price to compare with the pay-as-you go option common in the cloud. There is no simple solution, and different services have different dynamics. Some depreciate quickly while others do so more slowly. Moore's Law (a 1965 prediction that the number of transistors per silicon chip will double every year) makes it clear that basic IT services, like computing and storage, quickly lose value. In order to be certain that direct cost savings can be realized, total cost of ownership (TCO) calculations must be made for each service.

Indirect Cost Savings

If direct cost savings can be a bit tricky to calculate, the indirect ones are even more difficult. They stem primarily from increased efficiencies. A typical example is with database administrators, who will be able to manage x times more databases in the cloud because a lot of their typical tasks are handled by the cloud vendor. These types of efficiencies boost the work a typical employee can perform.

The most common way that efficiencies can be realized is by automating manual processes. This is a primary focus of DevOps, which most cloud vendors support. With DevOps, the process of deploying new applications and testing them can be automated to a certain extent, thereby saving system administrators and testers time.

Efficiencies are also gained from standardization. When those same technologies are used, it makes it easier to manage. This, however, is not attributable to the cloud as such, but more of a consequence of converging on-cloud technologies.

The major source of indirect cost savings has to do with the vendor assuming all the low-level management tasks, such as buying, setting up, and configuring servers and installing the software on them. The vendor will often be able to do that cheaper than the customer. Indirect cost savings are almost a guarantee in the cloud. If the vendor cannot save the customer cost via increased operational efficiencies, the move to the cloud is harder to justify.

Practical Guide to Leveraging the Economic Benefits of the Cloud

The previous sections discussed theoretical considerations. In practice, it may prove difficult to save money if the customer is not aware of how the cloud cost structure works. If one is not attentive, the theoretical advantage may quickly disappear, because practical implementation does not follow. Let's look at a few practical aspects of managing the cloud economy.

Cost Model

The first thing to be aware of is the structure of the cloud cost model. It can be quite foreign when you are used to an on-premise model, which is more predictable with up-front license fees and subsequent yearly support fees. As you learned earlier, a key tenet of the cloud is that you pay only for what you use according to metered usage. There is no up-front cost. This means that what precisely is metered can be of great importance to the total cost of ownership. The following list explains typical units used in the cloud. Some are similar to on-premise license purchases, but in the cloud they are not typically bought in advance. Instead, they scale with use.

- **Users**—This is a classic measure used extensively with on-premise software. This is typically combined with different user types that have different capabilities in the system. The price is usually differentiated according to these different types. The challenge in keeping the price down is to be precise about how many users need the different types of access. If everyone is given the most expensive type, it is likely to become too expensive. It consequently requires quite a bit of analysis to understand what the organization actually needs to provide to its different users.

- **Time**—One of the most common ways to meter usage is by the time used. Depending on the service, it can be hours, minutes, or even seconds. This is effective and quite intuitive. You are charged only when you are using the resource. Most infrastructure and platform services are metered in time. There may be tiers according to the functionality or processing power needed. The difference can be significant between lower tiers and higher ones. Similar to the user metric, it is therefore often important to precisely analyze what is needed in order not to pay too much.

- **Memory**—Although memory in general is becoming cheaper, it is still widely used. Naturally, this is particularly the case with storage-based services like databases. Services metered by memory are therefore rarely the ones that provide the biggest surprises.

- **Transactions**—Some services are metered by the number of transactions or rather by thresholds like millions of transactions. Naturally this is particularly used with transactional-type services like web services or messaging. This metric is not used when operating an on-premise IT setup, where the number of transactions does not make any difference. Moving to the cloud may require retooling the architecture to be less "chatty" in order to be cost-effective.

- **Custom**—There are other measures that are custom to an application. They might have something to do with the business flow, such as the number of leads or deals made. This is more prevalent in SaaS, where the service is closer to the business processes, but it may occur in lower-level cloud computing too.

- **Composite measures**—There are two types of composite measures. One is when two or more different measures are metered at the same time, such as storage and transactions. Another is when different measures are calculated together, such as the number of CPU cores, the power of the cores, time, and memory. Oracle and IBM used this measurement approach on-premise devices and have tried to carry them over to the cloud. They are particularly non-transparent and can only be ascertained after having watched the system perform for a while and determining its impact on cost.

Budgeting and Account Structure

As many critics of the cloud have pointed out, it can quickly become expensive to run IT in the cloud. That typically happens if you are not aware of who pays for what and why.

Structuring the accounts properly becomes more important the bigger the investment and the greater the commitment to the cloud. If the organization has a few teams that dabble with the cloud for experimentation and development purposes, it might be fine to go with the traditional one credit card, one account type. But if the organization has multiple units and wants to run production-grade workloads, it may be smart to consider how the account is structured. Should there be one for the entire organization, one for each business unit or team, or something else?

It might smart to have one account for the enterprise since the customer can negotiate discounts, but then it quickly becomes an issue as to how to split the bill internally. The different business units that use the cloud likely have their own budgets. Since cloud costs can easily run away if you are not attentive, it may be necessary to direct costs to where they are used. The cloud is not designed in the same way as on-premise license sales and support, whereby an invoice is sent to a specific cost center. There is one big invoice for everything. Furthermore, different services may have different purposes, which need to be outlined on the invoice.

Consequently, the challenge is to itemize the costs and channel them to the correct internal cost centers. This is typically achieved using tags, but it may still prove to be a challenge to the finance department to handle this type of invoice. You should determine in advance how your company will structure the cloud account and invoicing process to complement the organization's cost and accounting structure.

Cost Monitoring

Whether there is an actual budget or not, it might be good to work with budgets in the cloud. The budgets can be used to control spending in the cloud. A budget can be created for any number of services and rules can be set up to alert you when the threshold is approaching. For example, when 80% of the budget is reached. This is helpful even if there is no actual budget in a financial sense, but just an expectation that something will cost a specific amount. It is also possible to cut off the service once the budget threshold has been reached if economy is a key concern.

The cloud vendors have a variety of dashboards that provide good detail about current spending across services. If the tags are set up, one can also break it down by tags. Economic monitoring is thus only a question of how detailed you want to make it. Depending on the metadata you have configured, you can compile very detailed analysis on the use of the cloud across products, units, environments, or any other division.

Monitoring is also close to real time. Along with this insight, it will be possible to see projections of future use. Based on actual or prognosticated spending, you can configure alerts. This is a good failsafe idea, since it is easy to unintentionally activate services or forget to turn them off after use. It's very wise to establish at least some measures of cost monitoring, at the very least for the account.

Cost Optimization

As mentioned, the cloud is not automatically the cheaper option. Indeed, if you run the cloud the same way you run your on-premise data center, you are almost certain to incur higher expenses. It is necessary to use the following key cloud cost optimization techniques in order to successfully save money on the cloud.

- **Rightsizing**—Since you are paying for what you use, it is particularly important to figure out exactly what you *need* to use. Otherwise, you are quickly going to be paying for more than you need. This is not trivial. As an example, virtual machines (VMs) are priced depending on their specifications and nothing is free. This is why you need to find the right type of VM and the right size for each individual payload. If you do not, you are going to be paying more consistently.

- **Opening hours**—When you run an on-premise data center, having extra environments running day and night means extra electricity, which is comparably low. In the cloud, licenses are coupled with electricity and billed by the hour or minute. This means that every hour that something is up and running but not used is wasted money. Therefore, it may make sense to establish opening hours for non-production environments or even production environments. If system resources only need to be available on weekdays in the daytime, it is possible to save more than 60% by closing them down on evenings and weekends.

- **Right-time computing**—For some types of computing, the price varies over time and there may be cost reductions in waiting for non-time critical workloads. This is because resources are used more at certain times of the day than others, creating excess capacity at other times.

- **Storage classes**—Although storage has become cheap, it still costs money. This depends on how frequently data is accessed, the redundancy of the data, and other aspects. Again, knowing how your company wants to use storage for each use case can save you a lot of money.

- **Shut down unused resources**—In on-premise data centers it is not uncommon to have servers running idle. As mentioned, that costs electricity, which is a fraction of the metered usage per hour, since license costs are factored into that price. It therefore makes sense to identify idle resources and shut them down.

- **Make consumers accountable for costs**—Since it is very easy to spin up system resources and forget they are running, it is necessary to create incentives around limiting such unnecessary costs. This is best done by making the consumers accountable to the costs. That way they will know the economic consequences and factor that into their behavior.

- **Rearchitect for the cloud**—When workloads built for on-premise computing are moved to the cloud, it sometimes makes sense to re-architect them to better fit the cloud's cost structures. If a service is billed by number of transactions, for example, unnecessary transactions should be minimized or data-pooled into fewer transactions. If data structures involve a large amount of redundancies, some of these could be eliminated.

Summary

This chapter discussed how the cloud impacts the economy of IT assets. There are two ways this works to the customer's benefit: the cloud can increase revenue and decrease costs.

We covered three ways that the cloud could potentially increase revenue. The first was by making the company more agile; that is, be able to quickly adapt to changes in circumstances, such as sudden surges in usage or changes in the marketplace. The second was by increasing customer retention and the third was by helping to attract new customers, which can generate additional revenue.

As for reducing costs, we identified two ways the cloud can help: by reducing direct and indirect costs. The direct cost savings stem from less spending on comparable IT services, which leads to a lower total cost of ownership. The indirect cost savings stem from increased efficiencies in company operations.

We also reviewed some guidelines for reducing costs. First of all, it is necessary to consider the differences in the cloud cost models versus the traditional on-premise models. Second, one must consider how cloud costs fit into the company's accounting structures. Working with cloud computing requires a higher awareness of budgeting and cost monitoring.

In the end, we considered a few practical tips for how to keep costs down in the cloud. A general observation is that you need to be much more attentive to utilization and develop a deeper understanding of what is actually needed.

Working with the Cloud

This chapter focuses on how the cloud affects work. Since the cloud is expanding rapidly it is impacting all organizations in one way or another. The skills needed in the workforce are changing rapidly. Now cloud skills are in short supply.

Some tasks disappear, some remain, and new ones appear. Of the remaining ones, many are changing. A number of new roles appear, and old roles disappear or need to be adapted to work with the cloud. Some of these are core roles that always need to be in place for any significant cloud investment. Others are more specialized and apply only to certain types of organizations. Another thing to keep in mind is that traditional roles are being redefined, which necessitates retooling and an effort in training employees and getting them out of their comfort zones.

The chapter looks at how we can manage the transition to the cloud by considering how to acquire these new skills. It also provides a few practical guidelines for managing the impact on the organization.

© Anders Lisdorf 2021
A. Lisdorf, *Cloud Computing Basics*,
https://doi.org/10.1007/978-1-4842-6921-3_13

Changing Tasks in the Cloud

Like any technological revolution, there is an associated change in the work that needs to be done. For illustrative purposes, let's consider how the automobile revolutionized transportation and supplanted the horse and carriage as the primary mode of transportation.

Around the turn of the previous century, the horse and carriage were the undisputed champions of transportation. Industries and jobs were centered on the horse as transportation. The impact of the dominance of equine transportation can be seen across millennia and geography in hundreds of names and surnames. Rosalind, Farrier, Phillip, Marshall, Achaius, Cafferty, Ahern, Steadman, and Coltrane are all examples of names that relate to the horse and professions related to it. While the IT industry has not yet had the same impact on personal names, the change is in many ways similar.

In order for the horse to be a viable mode of transportation a great number of tasks had to be maintained. First of all, the horses had to be bred by breeders. They were kept and fed in stables. In order to keep going for long distances on the road, they needed metal shoes. In order to transport more people and goods, carriages were needed. Jobs and industries developed around the horse as a mode of transportation. Millions of people across the world made their living in the equine mobility industry.

When the automobile arrived, horse-based transportation was eliminated in the space of a couple of decades, and this had a perceptible impact on work. Some tasks were no longer needed. New tasks appeared such as filling the tank with gasoline and repairing the vehicle. Many tasks remained. Selling vehicles changed from carriages to automobiles. Driving changed from horse-drawn carriages to automobiles. Professions such as hackney carriages, originally a horse drawn for hire service, changed to automobiles and came to be known as taxies. Some tasks even remained unchanged. It was still necessary to collect the fare, hire drivers, and load the vehicles.

Impact on Tasks in the Cloud

Something similar to the transition from equine to automotive transportation is happening in the transition from on-premise to cloud systems. For example, database administrators will not have to do many of the tasks they do today, and server technicians don't need to unwrap boxes of servers and mount them into server racks, but both will have to do new things they are not doing today. There are completely new tasks that will appear, while others disappear. Another group of tasks remain in the cloud, some of them changed and some of them unchanged. We can chart this process in a grid (see Figure 13-1).

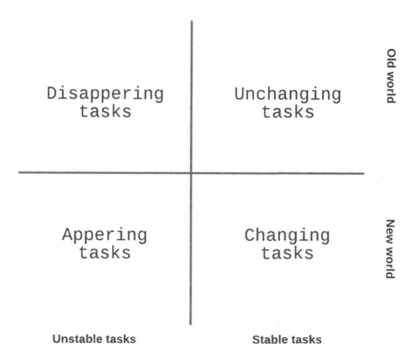

Figure 13-1. Tasks in the cloud

When managing information technology, there are thousands of different tasks, some very specific to certain technologies. Let's take a look at a few of the more widespread ones. These are just meant to give you a flavor of the types we are talking about.

Disappearing Tasks

Tasks are disappearing because they are no longer necessary due to the changing nature of the cloud. Consider the following tasks:

- Buying, receiving, and mounting servers in racks—A server is ordered from a vendor. When it is delivered, it's received and the papers are checked that the shipment is correct. Then the server is transported to the server room, unwrapped, plugged in, and mounted in a server rack.

- Decommissioning old hardware—When old hardware is replaced or breaks down, it needs to be disposed of. Frequently this is not a simple exercise since sensitive data may be on it. It also needs to be delivered to specific locations that take this kind of waste.

- Server room fire proofing—Servers can burn and since they operate on electricity and generate quite a lot of heat, it is necessary to establish additional fireproofing. Such installations are highly specialized and also need to be tested in fire drills every now and then.

- Physical security—Access to the physical servers needs to be managed in order to protect it from theft and breaches. Managing access to authorized personnel requires printing physical cards, assigning access codes, and setting up access rights.

- Upgrading software—When working on-premise, the software needs to be updated with a certain frequency. This includes everything from small patches to large system upgrades and even migrations. This is never necessary in PaaS or SaaS systems, but still might be necessary in some IaaS solutions.

- Database administration—Similarly speaking of PaaS databases, most tasks, such as managing table space and performance, go away along with upgrades. If the database is implemented in IaaS, these tasks remain. DBAs are still needed, though, in order to right-size and monitor the databases and test backup integrity.

New Tasks

These new tasks are necessary due to the cloud. These are new tasks that an organization did not do before it started using the cloud.

- Cost monitoring—As you learned earlier, it is necessary to have some degree of cost monitoring. Since cost is metered, usage is necessary to monitor in order to make sure costs do not escalate beyond control. This was not necessary in the on-premise world, since most costs were fixed. Licenses were paid up front and servers had a predictable cost. The only truly variable cost was electricity, but even that was limited since servers were on most of the time. In the cloud everything is variable, and you know it only after the fact. This is why cost monitoring is necessary.

- Account administration—This involves administering the structure of the account and who can do what in the cloud. Policies for use of services and infrastructure need to be in place and cost allocation needs to be set up. Security also has to be integrated into the cloud account's setup.

- Infrastructure automation—Infrastructure automation also exists on-premise, but in the cloud a lot of extra options exist. Since no human needs to be involved in procuring system resources, the procurement can be automated. For example, in relation to scaling or fail over in connection with a break down. Setting these rules up and then configuring and testing them is something new.

Unchanged Tasks

Some tasks do not go away when moving to the cloud. They do not even change. Let's consider those next:

- User administration—There are users in the cloud just as there are on-premise. They have usernames and passwords and/or keys, which is also the same. They still need to be created and maintained as always.

- Access control—Similarly, access control will be the same as on-premise. The same protocols and tools that are used here will be deployed against cloud systems. Single sign on and identity management will continue in the same form, with endpoints in the cloud.

- Support—When issues arise with systems, we will still need support in the cloud. Obviously, new support guidelines need to be developed and the staff will need to be trained, but that is true with any new technology.

- Writing code—Developers and engineers will still write code. Although certain areas that were previously only done with code can be done with point-and-click interfaces, or pseudocode as in the no-code trend catching on, the bulk of IT development will still remain driven by code. That code will be developed in the same IDEs and checked in and out of the same version control tools. In the cloud, they will be deployed to a server that's not physically running in the organization's data center.

- Change management—Managing changes to systems will remain a task in the cloud. If an error occurs, it needs resolution, and the process will be the same. If an upgrade or implementation is underway, it needs to follow the same procedure as any other upgrade or on-premise implementation.

Tasks that Changed

Some tasks remain, but have to be changed because of the cloud. The changes are substantial enough that you cannot do them without learning new skills, but still close enough that you can use existing knowledge.

- Monitoring systems—Even in the cloud, systems fail and knowing when this happens is still important. This is why they are monitored. The cloud also allows monitoring system resources, but it has to be set up differently. Tools particular to the cloud vendor need to be used and they differ from on-premise tools and between vendors.

- Provisioning—Making system resources available is still important, but whereas in an on-premise setting provisioning is typically done by an infrastructure team according to a request, in the cloud it can be done by anyone through self-service. Whether that is preferable or not is another question, but it is different than how it used to get done.

- Network configuration—Designing and configuring a network is a complex task for an on-premise data center involving routers, switches, and firewalls. It is no less complex in the cloud, but the tools and technologies may differ. It is still necessary to create network segments and rules for how traffic flows, but it is done in a different manner.

Roles in the Cloud

It can be difficult to get a grip on exactly what the changes in tasks mean in terms of human resources. The following sections describe the necessary roles. First, we look at core roles that any significant production-grade use of the cloud necessitates. After that follows a few specializations that are common but may not be needed in all cases. The relevance depends on the context. With all of them, it is possible to find training courses. In most cases, there are also certifications, at least that's the case for AWS, Azure, and Google.

Core Roles

There are a few roles that have to be in place regardless of how an organization uses the cloud, at least if it is used for anything more than experiments and trials. These roles need to be filled in order to maximize the chance of success.

Solution Architect

The solution architect is tasked with designing optimal, secure, and robust solutions based on the capabilities available in the cloud. That means the solution architect needs all-round knowledge of the cloud, the services that are available, and how to use them. This in itself can be a challenge since few IT professionals are comfortable with infrastructure, security, network, databases, and development frameworks. On top of this, a knowledge of architecture principles, good practice, and common architecture patterns for building optimal cloud-based solutions are to be expected.

These skills are all used to develop and specify the design that developers use to implement the solution. When the developers and specialists take over, the solution architect is relied on only for implementation guidance.

Developer

Developer are tasked with implementing the solutions the solution architect designed. Developers are also sometimes called engineers. They build, test, and maintain solutions.

This means that the bulk of the work has to do with writing code and configuring solutions in order to build a functioning system or component. In the cloud, the developer typically has more responsibilities than is common on-premise and may be relied on to deploy solutions. Debugging, logging, and defining metrics for monitoring the performance of the system are also the developer's responsibility.

The tools will typically be familiar ones to a developer, like command-line interfaces (CLI) for writing instructions, Software Development Kits (SDK) for building solution specific components, and Application Programming Interfaces (API) for interfacing with other solutions. Often it is possible to work in the same Integrated Development Environment (IDE) as they did on-premise. Only now it deploys to the cloud.

In general, the developer is responsible for application lifecycle management. In the cloud, there may be more responsibilities and thought must be given to certain cloud-specific issues like network and security, but apart from that, most of the work is fairly similar to the on-premise role.

Cloud Administrator

Cloud administrators deploy the systems and keep them running. This role is sometimes also called SysOps, because the role performs a variety of tasks that fall under operations. Once solutions have been developed and tested, they will be the responsibility of the cloud administrator. This means that traditional tasks, like deployment and monitoring, falls under the cloud administrator. They are also responsible for cost control mechanisms, such as setting up and monitoring usage and alerts.

Maintaining and implementing network configurations is a significant part of the job, since this is complex and has great consequences for resilience and security. This can get particularly challenging if the cloud is hybrid and needs to take into account on-premise network structure.

Security from an operational point of view is likewise an important task. This could include monitoring with alerts, different kinds of scans, patches, and audits of existing solutions.

The cloud administrator is in many ways similar to the system administrator of on-premise installations, but the tools are different and responsibilities may be wider.

Specializations

The specializations build on the core roles. They take particular aspects of their responsibility and focus on them. This means that specializations are used when certain aspects are especially important to the organization. For example, when a core function is using data for advanced analytical purposes, a data science specialist may be needed. Let's look at the most common specializations.

Data Science

Although data science seems like a regular coder like any other, it is in practice something different. Data scientists often employ a particular space between business and IT, since they work and have deep knowledge of business problems and data as well as advanced developer knowledge in certain respects. They also typically work with production data and build and maintain the solutions by themselves. Data science tools form an ecosystem of their own and are very specialized. A data scientist role needs to know the tools of the ecosystem and how to use them correctly.

Security

The security specialist focuses on validating the security of designs, configuring certain types of solutions associated with security and auditing existing. The security tools in the cloud are numerous and it is a constant area of development. This is why a specialist is sometimes employed. The security specialist needs to understand how the different solutions in the cloud work to protect solutions that run there. Some are diagnostic tools and others monitor and detect security issues.

Networking

Most organizations with significant on-premise infrastructure will have a networking unit that works full time only with networks. This is because it is important to protect the confidentiality and integrity of data. The same is the case in the cloud; the complexity and challenges do not go away. The networking specialist needs to understand networking in detail, including how it applies to the cloud. There is no difference between the standards, protocols, and functional components, since the Internet is just a network. What is different are the tools and the ways to achieve the result.

Database

The database specialist is not to be confused with a traditional DBA, who would administer a relational database. With the cloud, a great number of different types of databases have become available, as we saw earlier. The database specialist needs to understand how these different databases work, and what they are good for, as well as handling more complex tasks related to databases. For organizations with varied data needs, this can be an important role in order to optimize solutions.

DevOps

The DevOps specialist works with a combination of development and operations, which is the basis for the portmanteau DevOps. It has been a trend in agile development for a long time to implement solutions in production as fast as possible. This is achieved with DevOps. The specialist needs to understand the tools and configure them. A big part of this relies on processes and automation of infrastructure and the test system. Establishing the infrastructure and maintaining it falls under the responsibility of the DevOps specialist.

Managing the Changes in the Workforce

Adopting a cloud system means considerable change in the work that needs to be done and the roles therein, so there is a need to adapt the skills of the workforce. The new tasks in particular require attention in terms of developing relevant skills. There is a difference between the new and the changing tasks in the cloud in terms of learning. It may be easier to retrain resources for tasks that change rather than for completely new tasks. There are different training options available that we will consider.

There is also a more substantial organizational challenge in adapting the workforce to the cloud. Some employees will see the value of their skills diminished due to cloud adoption. They are not going to be obsolete from day to day, which means that they have to be retained. This means that the transition to the cloud also entails a significant organizational challenge, where large numbers of employees have to be retrained, laid off, or have their roles redefined. Conversely, since many new roles and skillsets need to be acquired by the organization, it must focus on how to attract new talent or train its existing employees.

Acquiring New Skills

Insofar as cloud skills are not something well known, they might need be learned or sourced somehow. The following sections discuss common ways to acquire cloud skills.

Online Resources

Today a number of good online resources exist that explain virtually any aspect of the cloud. In particular, topics related to specific certifications are widely available and are of good quality. Good and pedagogical videos exist for exam preparation for most of the cloud vendor certifications. These are found at the major online course providers, such as Udemy and Coursera. If the organization encounters a particular problem, it is similarly often possible to find either a video or description somewhere on GitHub, Stack Overflow, or similar.

Another good source of online resources are the cloud vendors themselves. They are interested in disseminating as much information as possible to help adoption of the cloud. Therefore, they will have a lot of good quality tutorials, labs, guidelines, wikis, whitepapers, and ebooks. The videos from their developer conferences are popular and inspiring and they also sometimes show practical demos and discuss customer cases.

Courses

Cloud vendors or their partners often provide courses in cloud-related subjects. All the roles mentioned previously can be found in one version or another, maybe with a slightly different title. It has also become common to have tiers, the most basic being practitioner, then associate, and then professional as the top tier. The cloud vendors also specify the sequence in which to take the courses.

Partner Training

Hiring an implementation partner or a skilled consultant with practical experience is another valid and popular alternative. This partner joins the cloud customer in hands-on implementation together with a team. They can give practical advice while working on the implementation. Such practical knowledge is hard to come by, since courses cover idealized cases, and tutorials and expert advice is idiosyncratic. This is an important way to ensure the practical knowledge needed to succeed is passed along.

Trial and Error

It is, of course, also possible to hack at it until it works. That is a tried-and-tested approach that has worked for decades. If there is no time or budget constraints, this is a decent model, since it encourages "organic" learning by letting developers explore and find solutions by themselves. It is not recommended if the goal is production-grade solutions. There is also a risk that bad habits may be learned from the beginning, thus undermining later progress.

Handling the Organizational Impact

As mentioned, a fundamental change in technology, like the cloud, is bound to create concern and unease among employees, whose livelihood and even identity is tied to the technology that's being replaced. When we see a technology change at the scale of the cloud, it is bound to have impact on a lot of employees' work and therefore their lives. Realizing this and planning for it up front is a good way to minimize the disruption down the line and make the transition to the cloud smoother.

Chart the Possible Impact on the Workforce

When an organization starts the journey toward the cloud—whether they go all in or do it more piecemeal—it will have an impact on the organization. The very fact of change in itself is bound to antagonize some people with a vested interest in maintaining the status quo. Moreover, some people are going to see their jobs become more or less obsolete, while others will need to change dramatically. Understanding these impacts is important in order to begin to address them positively.

The first step is to chart the tasks that will disappear. Finding out who does them today will give you an indication of who is at risk of losing their jobs. That is the most serious impact to handle and a decision needs to be made about what these people will be doing afterward. If they are being let go, it's a good idea to find incentives to keep them until the migration is complete. These people are often the only ones who know how the legacy technologies work and they are therefore critical to a smooth migration.

The next step is charting the tasks that will change. Those who perform these tasks today have to be kept informed about the plans and trained to continue to do their jobs in the cloud. Figuring out how to communicate to them and subsequently tailoring a training regime that will work is critical. This can be any combination of courses, online resources, and partner training, as you read earlier.

The final step is identifying the new tasks that will appear. Who will do those jobs going forward? Are internal people being retrained and reassigned? In that case, someone else has to be recruited to do their tasks. It could also be a case of recruiting new hires who are already qualified. Especially for the core roles it is important to have experienced personnel. Hiring for this can be tricky.

When moving to the cloud, it is necessary to identify the disappearing, changing, and new tasks. Determine how this all impacts the organization. Based on the findings, a plan can be made to adapt the workforce to the new demands.

Develop Career Paths for the Cloud

If the cloud investment is significant, it may be worthwhile to develop career paths for employees. In the current job market, it may prove difficult to rely on recruiting externally if the organization is not already at the top tier. A more sustainable approach is to plan for careers in the cloud from the outset. Developing career paths can help communicate the direction and expectations, as well as help retain existing employees.

Career paths that focus on the core roles and lead to specializations is one way to approach it, since more people are going to be used in the core roles.

Redefine Identities and Communication

Since work is often a big part of an individual's identity, helping employees redefine their jobs can add to job satisfaction. Rather than communicating and conceptualizing the cloud as something opposed to and better than the existing process, it may make sense to try to communicate it as a continuation.

Implementing the cloud involves a lot of meetings, maybe even seminars or town halls. For these purposes, it is a good idea to be attentive to how the cloud is communicated. Building an inclusive story about organic change is better than one of disruptive leaps of efficiency. Not the least because such leaps are rare in real life.

Close the Skills Gap

As mentioned, there are many ways to close the skills gap when transitioning to the cloud. The first decision is whether to maintain the skills in-house. If the organization relies critically on IT, as for example building technology products or maintaining websites, an in-house model could be worthwhile. The choice is then whether to train the existing workforce or source externally. Sometimes there is not much choice, since it can be very hard to recruit if the organization is not well known or doesn't pay well. It may therefore be a necessity to build on internal resources. A good model here is to focus on employees who are generalists or juniors who have not specialized yet. The cloud is equally new to anyone and has to be learned. Focusing on training people may be a good way to motivate and retain them.

Alternatively, skills can be sourced externally. It is easier and quicker to find skilled resources with consultancies. They can usually find the roles needed. A choice has to be made between near shore or offshore resources. There may be better availability and a better price for offshore resources, but it comes at a cost of more difficult coordination. Near shore resources are typically more expensive but are easier to engage and embed as parts of a team. These are necessary for the partner model, where an experienced consultant participates in the daily work and supplies hands-on expertise and training. In theory, this could be done with offshore resources too, but coordination and experience about the customers everyday challenges are difficult if you are not onsite.

The solution could also be a hybrid one, where core roles are insourced, and specializations are outsourced. It could also be development that is outsourced, whereas operations and security are insourced. These choices depend on the business model and the organization's priorities.

Summary

This chapter discussed how the cloud impacts the work people do. The transition from an equine to an automotive mobility sector created new jobs, made some disappear, and changed others. The cloud also brings with it significant changes in the work that needs to be done. We saw a few examples of these tasks.

The roles in the cloud can be divided into core roles and specializations. Core roles always need to be in place in order to manage any significant investment in the cloud, and specializations depend on the nature and priorities of the company.

These changes are bound to affect the workforce and have to be managed. Work has a great influence on identity and happiness and changes may therefore affect employee well being and churn. The impact of the cloud on the organization must be charted and planned for.

Understanding the mix of opportunities to train the workforce is important in order to develop the right incentives and skills. Finally, we reviewed a number of recommendations for how to adapt the workforce to future needs in the cloud with minimal disruption.

Adopting the Cloud

We have looked at the history of the cloud, discussed its primary vendors, and learned how the four aspects of technology, security, economy, and work differ on the cloud versus on-premise IT. This chapter focuses on how organizations can adopt the cloud. Although every company is unique, there are a lot of commonalities. There are several things that are similar across industries and types of organizations. Instead of having to start from a blank page, we look at what others in similar situations have done to adopt cloud computing at the organizational level. Based on these examples, we provide a number of patterns of adoption that have proven successful.

Not all organizations can spring forth as cloud native like the hyped startups that capture the agenda of cloud computing so far. Most companies are much more selective and constrained in their adoption. This chapter describes how organizations can approach cloud adoption in a structured and proven way and find an adoption pattern that matches their particular needs. The goal is therefore to describe the most common ways organizations can approach cloud computing.

© Anders Lisdorf 2021
A. Lisdorf, *Cloud Computing Basics*,
https://doi.org/10.1007/978-1-4842-6921-3_14

Patterns of Adoption

In tech it is popular to talk about patterns. Whether it is development, integration, or even a PowerPoint presentation, they have their books about patterns. This way of thinking was originally developed in architecture by Christopher Alexander, who had an ambition to develop a pattern language for architecture. A *pattern* is an optimal solution to a recurring problem. In Alexander's thinking, patterns exist at different levels, from the macro level of city planning, down to the micro level of detailed design. Similarly, patterns of cloud adoption have already been documented at many levels. Primarily for low-level design. Vendors like AWS and Azure have done a great job at documenting many best practice solutions to problems in the form of patterns. What we look at here is an attempt at describing the patterns at the highest level of cloud adoption, which is analogous to city planning. Only here the city is an organization and the buildings are IT solutions.

The format we use to describe the patterns is the following:

- **Context**—In what context does the need for the pattern arise? This is a description of the situation in which the pattern should be used.

- **Problem**—What is the problem the pattern addresses? This is a concise description of the typical problem the pattern seeks to solve.

- **Forces**—What are the key forces? These are the most important factors that affect the pattern.

- **Solution**—What is the solution to problem? This is a description of what can be done to overcome the problem.

- **Example**—What is an example? This is an illustration of a solution using this pattern.

- **Related patterns**—What patterns may come before or after? Some patterns naturally follow or precede others.

Using patterns is not an exact science. They should be used for inspiration. Don't be so tied to a certain pattern that you develop something that does not fit the needs of your organization. Patterns also carry with them challenges that we will highlight.

Cloud-Native

We frequently hear about companies that are completely cloud-based and it seems to be the default for cloud vendors. We see this in the examples shown at conferences and whitepapers. These companies often have a product that is in itself cloud-based and they are often startups and relatively young companies. The Cloud-Native pattern is one where all IT runs in the cloud. This is natural for everyone in the organization. This pattern is often the frame of reference in marketing material and examples mentioned at vendor conferences.

- **Context**—An organization without any existing on-premise solutions needs to build functional solutions quickly. This is often a new company, but could also be a company that has moved everything to the cloud.

- **Problem**—How do you build state-of-the-art software without a big infrastructure and operations unit and without major investments in hardware? The key here is that the organization does not want to tie capital and recruiting expertise to run on-premise infrastructure operations.

- **Forces**—There is a need to adapt quickly to changing surroundings. The competitive landscape may be shifting quickly, but it could also be due to other forces, such as consumer preferences, regulatory demands, or technological changes. Another force is cost efficiency, whereby investments in IT need to be optimized. This can mean finding something cheaper, but it could just as well be a quest for something better at a comparable price.

- **Solution**—Choose a cloud vendor that can support all immediate application needs. Make use of PaaS and serverless solutions where possible, since they require less operational attention. A variant could be to have a multi-cloud approach. That requires a decision on standards in order to be able to shift workloads around. Establish one central cloud-based IAM solution in order to have full control of access to computing. The same is the case for Application Lifecycle Management, where key functions like versioning, deployment, and service management should similarly converge on a single solution if more than one cloud vendor will be used. In general, the Cloud-First pattern needs some standardization and governance.

- **Example**—An example of a cloud-native company is Pinterest. It delivers a cloud-based product and is completely based in the cloud. But interestingly, it did not start that way. It shifted completely to the cloud in 2017, seven years after its inception.

- **Related patterns**—The Cloud-Native pattern can be preceded by the Lift and Shift pattern, as with Pinterest, and the Anarchy pattern, where a multitude of cloud-based solutions are standardized and put into a more systematic fashion.

The Cloud-Native pattern is rarely the approach for established companies with more than a few years of history. This is because they will typically already have a significant amount of systems on-premise. Although this pattern is used for demonstrations and marketing, it is often misleading to think it should be followed, since most companies are not in a position where it makes sense. That would require them to convert the entire IT staff to cloud experts. Therefore, one should be aware of this pattern and consider whether it is truly a good match, that is whether the context is really the same. For newly founded companies, cloud-native should be the default pattern. There is no reason not to start as cloud-native.

One of the challenges of the cloud-native solution is to establish the same level of standardization and governance typically associated with on-premise IT. In the cloud, everyone can do everything, which is not the case for an on-premise infrastructure. This means that stronger governance and controls need to be actively put in place. The point is to avoid undermining operational stability, security, and economy. Another challenge, especially in a multicloud scenario, is how you oversee the organization's infrastructure. If solutions are spread out across multiple cloud vendors, it is a challenge to monitor them effectively. Duplicative functionality might occur more easily, which adversely impacts the total costs.

Cloud-First

Cloud-First differs from the Cloud-Native pattern in that it does not require any current IT to be in the cloud. The Cloud-First pattern just requires a decision about the cloud as the default option for all IT needs. It can be used by any organization, regardless of its current expertise or investment in IT. It also does not require IT to be in the cloud. Not even for new development. It just requires the cloud to be the first option whenever changes such as new development, upgrades, or modernization are undertaken.

- **Context**—An organization or business unit wants to take advantage of the cloud as quickly as possible without committing to migrating existing solutions. It can be anything from a startup to big mature organizations that have decided that the only thing that makes sense in the future is the cloud.

- **Problem**—How do you start reaping the advantages of the cloud as quickly as possible?

- **Forces**—The need to adapt quickly to changing surroundings is a powerful driver. Another is cost efficiency, since the cloud requires less capital expenditure and up-front investment.

- **Solution**—Establish a policy that all new IT development by default should be based on cloud solutions. The same should be the case for application modernization and upgrades. This means that while the cloud is the first option for new development, it needs not be the only option. If there are good reasons not to use the cloud that are legitimate, on-premise alternatives exist. This solution also makes no assumptions about legacy technologies actively being moved to the cloud.

- **Example**—New York City decided to go to a cloud-first strategy in 2017 in order to reap cost savings and efficiency gains. For all new development projects, the cloud was the first choice. Only if an adequate cloud solution could not be designed, would another solution be used. This had no consequences for existing services, which continued to run as they had before. But it impacted new projected systems and all modernization efforts.

- **Related patterns**—The Experimental pattern can be used to gain experience with the cloud and assess whether it might be the direction to go in the future. It can be followed or supplemented with the Incremental Change pattern in order to convert the remaining systems to cloud-based ones.

The Cloud-First pattern can be used effectively by any organization convinced that the cloud is the future. This is all it takes. It is easy to get started with and can quickly lead to improvements in terms of cost efficiency, scalability, and security.

The challenge is that it does little to change existing infrastructure. Only if an upgrade or modernization needs to be made will it impact legacy solutions, which means that it is not a final solution. Efforts must still be made to continue to run on-premise data centers. It can also bifurcate the technology organization into those that work on the old systems and those who work on new ones, which is unfortunate and may lead to lower levels of internal cooperation.

Lift and Shift

For IaaS in particular, the cloud offers a one-to-one alternative to running an on-premise data center. This can be done more securely and efficiently, cheaper, and in a more resilient manner. This is why it makes sense to lift and shift on-premise infrastructure to the cloud. The Lift and Shift pattern is well suited for low-hanging fruit, where very little if any changes need to be made in order to move from on-premise to the cloud.

- **Context**—An organization wants to minimize on-premise infrastructure in order to reduce infrastructure and operations costs and/or increase resilience and scalability in their infrastructure offering.

- **Problem**—How can you reduce cost and overhead in provisioning and maintaining basic IT infrastructure services?

- **Forces**—The primary driver is cost reduction in operating existing IT assets, but increased resilience is also a common driver. On-premise IT operations have high overhead on offering standard infrastructure services at an SLA compared to the cloud.

- **Solution**—Choose a cloud vendor compatible with the legacy software stack and establish a direct connection to the cloud vendor's data center. This will extend the on-premise data center with a virtual one. Move all standardized elements, like VMs and databases, to the cloud using a gradual lift and shift process that maintains the existing solution with little or no changes.

- **Example**—Netflix started its journey to the cloud in 2008 by moving its databases and VMs to the cloud. They simply could not have racked the servers fast enough to keep up and they experienced breakdown due to errors in upgrades.

- **Related patterns**—A related pattern is the Offload pattern, which concerns lower-level infrastructure offerings. Lift and Shift also works with standardized applications like databases. The Lift and Shift pattern may be followed by the Incremental Change pattern, which deals with more complex application stacks.

Lift and Shift is a good pattern for demonstrating results quickly and is commonly used for the low-hanging fruit. It will not give you all the benefits since you are just moving an on-premise application with no changes, but that can be fixed later with the Incremental Change pattern, for example. Lift and Shift is also comparatively easier since it works on basically the same operating model as on-premise, which reduces friction in adoption.

One caveat is that in order to reap the full benefits of the cloud in the long run, some thought should be put into the architecture and governance of the hybrid setup that will be the result. The challenge is to avoid on-premise habits in the cloud and to reassess the true needs and use tools available and best practices in the cloud.

Offload

Offloading to the cloud is similar to the Lift and Shift pattern in principle, since both work inside the on-premise paradigm. It has to do with extending existing infrastructure to the cloud in a seamless manner. That means that it involves basic infrastructure services like storage, network, and compute.

- **Context**—An organization with a large existing investment in basic infrastructure, such as virtual machines, file servers, storage, and backup want a cheaper, more secure, scalable, or efficient way of running existing infrastructure.

- **Problem**—How do you build robust infrastructure solutions that will support an existing diversified systems portfolio?

- **Forces**—Cost reduction and resilience are common motivations for choosing the Offload pattern.

- **Solution**—Choose a cloud vendor with a mature infrastructure capability and establish a direct connection to utilize standard infrastructure solutions for backup, virtual machines, SAN, NAS, and similar. The on-premise infrastructure can be extended through this connection to provide on-demand access to infrastructure.

- **Example**—An example is Airbus, which were building a new platform that would provide customers access to satellite images. These images comprise many hundreds of terabytes and are expanding continually. In order to offload the constant need for storage expansion, object storage was used.

- **Related patterns**—The Experimental pattern can be a precursor to choosing the Offload pattern, but it is simple enough to be a logical starting point for many companies that want to free up resources in IT infrastructure. A logical continuation is the Lift and Shift pattern, where applications are moved to the cloud.

The Offload pattern can be used with success where scalability of basic infrastructure is or has become a problem. It can be used in a detached manner, without any large commitment to the cloud. It's done in a more ad hoc fashion and therefore also can be used by primarily on-premise organizations. The challenge is that it does not actually move the organization closer to harvesting the full benefits of the cloud and may result in continuing the on-premise mentality and culture.

Regional Autonomy

Cloud adoption may not be homogeneous across an organization. Some types of organizations do not lend themselves well to centralization and standardization and have more autonomous business units that may not necessarily agree on how or if the cloud should be used. This type of organization often has a compartmentalized information and application infrastructure and typically optimizes around business unit output rather than looks for synergies and standardization across the organization. This calls for an approach that favors a high degree of autonomy.

- **Context**—An organization has a number of semi- or fully-autonomous business units. Every unit optimizes internally and is not rewarded for cross-organizational synergies, but is held accountable only for its own output. It will typically be in a competitive and dynamic market setting. It could also be the result of frequent mergers and acquisitions. If divisions operate in niches, these may have very particular requirements.

- **Problem**—How can you quickly and dynamically adapt IT to swift changes in the market and ecosystem?

- **Forces**—Fast changing market demands require rapid responses and quick turnaround, from idea to finished product.

- **Solution**—Let business units establish their own accounts at their cloud vendor of choice. Let them find out which vendor and services best solve a given problem for them. Do not standardize on technology but on interfaces for the IT that needs to be shared. Use microservices, streaming, and data virtualization to create uniform interfaces on heterogeneous technologies. Converge on a few core services that are shared, such as multicloud management solutions, application monitoring, access management, security, and cloud cost management.

- **Example**—The energy company Uplight was the result of a merger of six companies, each with a different technology stack. They decided that was fine, but implemented a central cloud-based Identity and Access Management (IAM) solution as a core service. This made the secure use of different solutions across entities safe and seamless.

- **Related patterns**—The Anarchy pattern can precede this pattern, in which case there is a transition to somewhat more structure in the Regional Autonomy pattern. The Experimental pattern can also lead to this pattern being chosen, at least initially, for the fastest adopting business units.

The Regional Autonomy pattern often is a de facto default pattern since business units are adopting cloud services regardless of what the centralized IT function wants. The cloud has only exacerbated this development, since business units are increasingly buying cloud services unilaterally. But there is a difference between how things are and how they should be. Therefore, it is important to check if your context is right for this pattern. Often it is not the case and the pattern should be changed to one that supports the organizational context and goals.

One of the primary challenges with this pattern is that it is wasteful and frequently duplicative in terms of capabilities implemented across the organization. That is the tradeoff made for speed and autonomy, which should be held up against the additional costs. For organizations that are characterized by autonomous business units, this pattern would support faster implementation and commitment to the cloud. Focus should be on the minimal functions and services that should be shared and allowing maximum freedom for everything else.

Incremental Change

Most organizations are more than a few years old and have a substantial investment in a diverse portfolio of on-premise technologies—legacy technologies if you will. For these types of organizations, the Cloud-Native pattern is simply not possible, and the Cloud-First pattern does not solve the basic challenge, that is, modernizing the on-premise technology needed for continuous operation. The Incremental Change pattern provides a path for gradually switching IT from on-premise to the cloud.

- **Context**—An organization with many years in the market and a diversified on-premise technology portfolio wants to modernize its IT assets in order to harness the new possibilities of the cloud. It frequently finds itself in situations where support runs out on technologies or upgrades of legacy infrastructure become prohibitively costly. The organization might also be tired of high software costs for basic technologies.

- **Problem**—How to selectively migrate to the cloud, with maximal value and minimal risk and investment?

- **Forces**—Reducing cost in the medium to longer term is a powerful driver of this pattern, but there's often also a general wish for modernization. Another potential force is a desire for standardization.

- **Solution**—Build a portfolio of potential use cases and projects where the cloud might be used. Select the best ones based on a scoring model that takes into account the organization's strategic objectives. Look for low-hanging fruit and avoid mission-critical and high-risk workloads initially. It is better to select easier projects first even if their total value is not the highest because this will provide the organization with learning points and experience. Many of the inevitable obstacles of moving to the cloud are better met with relatively inconsequential projects. This will also help build momentum and confidence around the cloud in the organization.

- **Example**—A large organization with tens of thousands of employees had many legacy applications and wanted to move its applications to the cloud. They decided to start with the HR system because it was relatively unconnected and easy to migrate to a cloud-based one. HR was not the most valuable to move, but based on this, the basic infrastructure was built in the cloud. The more complex ERP application would follow and could benefit from the lessons learned in the first, less consequential, migration.

- **Related patterns**—The Lift and Shift pattern will often precede or be used in conjunction with the Incremental Change pattern, as they both address ways to migrate legacy, on-premise application workloads to the cloud. Whereas Lift and Shift is a cruder way to move workloads with no or few changes, the Incremental Change balances each case against possibilities and objectives. When everything has been migrated to the cloud, the Cloud-Native pattern follows.

Incremental Change fits well with organizations that are not able to focus fully on cloud migration. Migrating in a more piecemeal fashion also allows the organization to gradually adapt, both in terms of developing the right skills and changing the culture. The flipside of this is that it is slow and may result in a lot of deliberation and discussion. This will slow down the transition to the cloud. Therefore, the benefits may not be quickly visible and can lead to doubt about moving to the cloud.

Anarchy

Some organizations just need to get something done as quickly as possible regardless of cost, quality, synergies, and alignment with organizational policies. Small teams reign supreme in the company culture. While Anarchy might sound negative, it is by far the most efficient in developing and executing new ideas quickly. The Anarchy pattern may therefore fit well with an organization that is in a hypergrowth phase or dependent on generating new and innovative solutions. We find many startups that fit this profile, but it also fits most research labs and data science teams. R&D-heavy companies similarly can use this pattern.

- **Context**—An organization where all that matters are the products of development teams. Survival of the company may depend on its ability to create new solutions. Software is not seen as an asset that needs to be protected, maintained, and developed, but rather as a means to an end that can be thrown away subsequently.

- **Problem**—How can one optimize idea development and delivery speed of a software solution?

- **Forces**—The primary force is time to market, since survival may depend on it. This is equally true of a research center, an early stage startup, or a biotech company. All crucially depend on being the first to discover or develop something. A secondary force is stimulating creativity and innovation. Requesting and waiting for IT resources may hinder and block the creative process.

- **Solution**—Every individual or small team gets its own credit card and can use it to sign up for any cloud service it finds helpful in whatever eclectic manner. No questions asked. Teams or even individuals adopt technology that best fits their needs, based on their own experience and familiarity. Converging on shared technologies will take precious time. If data scientists need to produce models, it is better that they choose whatever tool they need to build these models since they are only evaluated on the efficacy and value of them.

- **Related patterns**—The Regional Autonomy pattern is a related pattern and often follows. For example, in the case where an early stage startup develops into a more mature startup that does not have to fight for its life every day and needs to become more stable. It is the same process in biotechnology, where later stages of drug development require more predictable functions, such as regulatory affairs and compliance. Research-heavy institutions, such as universities, also typically have to tame the anarchy of research groups that have been run autonomously. This can be done with a Regional Autonomy pattern. The Incremental Change pattern may also offer a way to standardize and stabilize solutions. Even if they are already in the cloud, they carry a lot of technical debt much like legacy code.

The Anarchy pattern is well suited for idea generation. That does not mean it helps generate ideas, only the right employees will. It helps by radically moving all obstacles to generating new ideas and quickly implementing new solutions. This is also why it helps deliver solutions quickly: all checks and balances have been removed.

That also means that not much or any thought is given to robust operation and production-grade workloads. A lot of technical debt will be produced with this pattern and knowledge is tied to key employees. The consequence is that the risk profile is higher, and a large portion of the solution may need to be rebuilt in order to be secure, stable, or scalable enough for the longer term.

Experimental

The journey to the cloud has to start somewhere and providing a happy playground for experimentation can prove important for the future direction of cloud adoption. This can be done by different teams in parallel. The Experimental pattern aims to provide access to the cloud in an easy and safe manner for exploratory purposes.

- **Context**—An organization wants to start using the cloud without a strategic commitment. Before making such a commitment, they want to learn more. It could also be an organization moving into a new area, like IoT or machine learning, which is not presently offered by their on-premise IT.

- **Problem**—How can an organization find out if cloud computing can be used to add new capabilities or improve existing ones?

- **Forces**—Modernization of IT infrastructure and general application offering is a powerful force. Learning about technical trends and opportunities is another.

- **Solution**—Choose a cloud vendor and set up an isolated trial account that teams and individuals can access in order to do POCs and pilot implementations. Make sure that the setup has guard rails, so the users can't make any fatal mistakes. That involves budget limits, no connection to on-premise infrastructure, and no production data, for example. The primary purpose is to provide a safe space for experimentation that allows users to become confident with the technologies. Don't invest a lot of time and money in configuring multiple environments or deployment pipelines or integration to central IAM solutions. That may all have to change anyway based on the results of the experiments developers will make. It can be used for nonessential solutions but not production, which is something that should be communicated up front to users. The understanding is that everything can be terminated at will or with a short warning.

- **Related patterns**—Most of the other patterns considered in this chapter may follow naturally after the Experimentation pattern, since it helps determine which pattern fits the organization.

The Experimental pattern is a good starter pattern for organizations with little or no direct experience with the cloud. It teaches developers how the cloud works and removes doubt and uncertainty. It also helps them try out new ideas. In bigger organizations, the pattern can be continually used in new units that are being onboarded to the cloud, but gradually it will change into a development environment.

The biggest drawback is that it may remain just a playground used infrequently if no effort is being made to gather the lessons learned in some way. Point-and-click exploration is fine, but will rarely lead to anything substantial. In order to mitigate this, real POCs should be encouraged along with documentation of the lessons learned, which should be shared in the organization.

Summary

We have seen that cloud adoption is unlikely to be done in the same way by all organizations. Companies find themselves in different situations and therefore need different solutions.

At the organizational level, we considered a number of different patterns. These are not exhaustive, but represent a majority of the ways that organizations approach the cloud. Figure 14-1 shows a schematic of the relationship between them. Most adoption journeys start with the Experimental pattern, but any pattern can be the starting point.

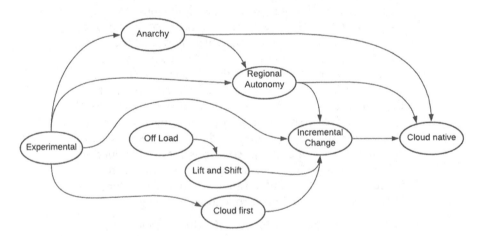

Figure 14-1. Relationship between patterns

The arrows in Figure 14-1 signify the logical direction of change. It would, for example, be strange for a company to move from a Cloud-Native pattern to an Incremental Change pattern. Although it is not impossible, as in the case of a merger with another company with significant legacy code, it is not common. These relationships can also help organizations map the journey through the cloud. The journey may start by using the Offloading pattern, then moving to Lift and Shift, and from there to the Incremental Change pattern. Eventually that could lead to a Cloud-Native pattern when everything has been moved. That is one typical development path for a mature company.

Startups will typically follow a different route. They often start with the Anarchy pattern as they fight for survival and are innovating, and then move to the Regional Autonomy pattern, which provides more stability, and finally end in a more stable Cloud-Native pattern.

For some companies, a complete move to the cloud may not be feasible or helpful. In that case, a pattern that supports a hybrid solution will be the endpoint rather than the Cloud-Native pattern. This is also fine, but modern companies are bound to use the cloud to some degree.

When adopting the cloud, it is important to choose a pattern that fits the organization's own context and direction, not simply one that's popular or presented at conferences. Once the right pattern or patterns have been chosen, the key is to execute them. This includes its own challenges since the approach has to be communicated and disseminated to the organization. One of the most common issues with cloud adoption is that the organization remains stuck in an on-premise mindset. This applies to all four main aspects—technology, security, economy, and work. In order to be efficient, the adoption journey therefore has to be accompanied by a culture change as well.

I

Index

A

Access control lists (ACLs), 138

Active Directory (AD), 137

AltaVista, 86

Amazon
    dot-com crash, 77, 78
    IaaS, 80
    origin, 75–77
    profile, 81–83
    reorientation, 78, 79
    S3, 80

Amazon Web Service (AWS), 80

American National Standard Institute
    (ANSI), 58

Anarchy pattern, 180

Application Programming Interfaces
    (API), 161

Application services, 122

Artificial intelligence (AI), 55

Azure, 72

B

Bare-metal server, 115

Berkeley Software Distribution (BSD), 39

Business Process as a Service (BPaaS), 15

Business processes, 132

Business to business (B2B), 127

Business to consumer (B2C), 127

C

Capital expenditures (CAPEX), 23

Cloud
    birth, 4
    core roles, 160–162
    definition, 1
    electronic box, 2
    metaphor, 2
    nodes, 2
    origin, 2, 3
    specializations
        database, 163
        data science, 162
        DevOps, 163
        networking, 163
        security, 163
    tasks, 157
        changed, 160
        disappearing, 157, 158
        new tasks, 158, 159
        unchanges, 159
    utility
        comparison, 14, 15
        configuration, 12
        path dependency, 11
        product, 11
        regulation, 13
        service continuity, 13
        transferability, 12
    workforce, changes
        courses, 165
        online resources, 164

© Anders Lisdorf 2021
A. Lisdorf, *Cloud Computing Basics*,
https://doi.org/10.1007/978-1-4842-6921-3

Printed in the United States
by Baker & Taylor Publisher Services